THE IRISH QUIZ BOOK

JIM BLACK

First published in 2000
The Appletree Press Ltd.,
The Old Potato Station
14 Howard Street South
Belfast BT7 1AP
Tel: (0) 28 90 243074
Fax: (0) 28 90 246756
Web Site: www.appletree.ie
E-mail: reception@appletree.ie

A catalogue record for this book
is available from the British Library.

The Irish Quiz Book

ISBN 0-86281-785-4

10 9 8 7 6 5 4 3 2

QUESTIONS

Geography

answers on page 138

1. The Ox Mountains in Mayo are also known as?

2. Where is Ireland's tallest round tower?

3. Shannon Airport is situated between which rivers?

4. Where is 'the lake isle of Innisfree'?

5. What is the lighthouse above Whitehead on the Antrim coast?

6. Which lough lies below Lough Conn?

7. Which lough lies between Loughs Corra and Corrib?

8. How many columns make up the Giant's Causeway?

9. Which rock makes up each of the columns in the Causeway?

10. How many counties are there in Northern Ireland?

11. How many counties are there in the Republic of Ireland?

12. What is the most northerly county in Ireland?

13. What is the main catch in Lough Neagh?

14. Which famous river runs through Dublin?

15. Which new counties were created in 1608?

History

answers on page 138

1. Which pretender to the English throne was crowned in Dublin?

2. Who founded the settlement which became Dublin?

3. What was the Inauguration Stone of the Irish kings?

4. Where was Sir Arthur Wellesley, later Prime Minister, born?

5. During which years did the Irish Potato Famine take place?

6. According to the Julian calendar, what was the date of the Battle of the Boyne?

7. Which rebellion is remembered by Slaughterford Bridge on Islandmagee and Bloody Bridge near Newcastle in Co. Down?

8. Which north Antrim ruin was the home of Cormac Cearnac, one of the famous Red Branch Knights of Ulster?

9. Who led the United Irishmen in rebellion in 1798 in Antrim, only to be hanged in Cornmarket in Belfast?

10. Which organisation was Wolfe Tone prominent in?

11. Thurgesius was king of which people?

12. When was the border between Northern Ireland and the Republic of Ireland agreed?

13. Which system of justice had been considered as an alternative to British law in Ireland during 1919-21?

14. Who was elected MP for North Tipperary in 1875, only to lose his seat as he was an escaped convict?

15. Which of Queen Elizabeth I's favourites once owned Lismore Castle, Co. Waterford?

Sport

answers on page 138

1. Snooker World Champion Dennis Taylor comes from which town in Co. Tyrone?

2. Which sport do Finn Harps play?

3. Which Irish sport is sometimes confused with the Scottish game shinty?

4. Mary Peters won Olympic Gold in which athletics event in 1972?

5. What was the final score in the first proper Hurling Final under G.A.A. rules in 1887?

6. What was the original title of the GAA, the Gaelic Athletic Association?

7. Which Irish horseracing trainer won the Irish 1,000 Guineas, Irish 2,000 Guineas, Irish St Leger, Irish Derby, King George VI and Queen Elizabeth stakes in 1963?

8. Which sport was involved in, but absent from, the formation of the GAA?

9. Where was the formation meeting of the GAA held?

10. Which two countries were awarded Olympic Bronze in the Lightweight division in 1964?

11. In which team sport did Ireland win Silver in 1908 Olympics?

12. Which team does Irish international footballer Ian Harte play for?

13. What is Limerick's main rugby venue?

14. Name the counties represented at formation of the Ladies Gaelic Football Association?

15. What is forbidden in Ladies' Football?

Politics
answers on page 138

1. When was the first recorded Irish parliament?

2. In which sport was Jack Lynch an outstanding player before entering political life?

3. Which Irish nationalist published *The Re-conquest of Ireland* in 1915?

4. Which state office did WB Yeats hold in 1922?

5. Who founded the Society of the United Irishmen?

6. Who was leader of Clan na Poblachta?

7. What was the title of the Irish Volunteers newspaper?

8. When did the first woman win a seat in the House of Commons?

9. When did she take her seat?

10. When was President Douglas Hyde born?

11.The Irish flag is similar in design (but in the opposite order) to that of which African nation?

12. "I found Ireland on her knees… Ireland is now a nation". Which politician said this?

13. Where was the birth-place of the Irish President from 17th June 1959?

14. What is the role of the ceann comhairle in Irish politics?

15. Which Irishman became Austrian governor of Dalmatia?

Literature

answers on page 139

1. Name the writer of the book on which the film *The Commitments* was based?

2. What is the name of Frank McCourt's follow-up memoir to *Angela's Ashes*?

3. What was the title of Bram Stoker's first novel?

4. Which Roddy Doyle novel won the Booker Prize winner in 1993?

5. When was James Joyce born?

6. When was *Ulysses* first published?

7. Which philosopher, born in Dublin, published *Philosophical Inquiry into the Origin of our Ideas of the Sublime and Beautiful* in 1756?

8. Which work by James Joyce became the novel, *A Portrait of the Artist as a Young Man*?

9. Which Irish poet's works include *The Poetry of WB Yeats*?

10. Why is the *Book of the Dun Cow* so-called?

11. Scrapings from early Irish books were said by the historian Bede to be effective against which threat to life?

12. What was CS Lewis' full name?

13. Who is the main character in *The Cattle Raid of Cooley*?

14. What does the *Book of Kells* contain?

15. Which Bernard McLaverty book was made into a film starring Liam Neeson as a priest?

Irish Language

answers on page 139

1. What was the Tain Bo Cualigne?

2. Who or what was the ard-rí?

3. What is 'Luan'?

4. Which month in Irish is Bealtaine?

5. What is 'rugby' in Irish?

6. What does 'fada' mean in English?

7. What does 'fainne' mean in English?

8. What does a 'fada' do to a vowel?

9. What is the Oireachtas?

10. What was an 'ollamh'?

11. Which animal is called 'grainneog' in Irish?

12. What is a neamhóg?

13. What is 'Chumann Sléibhteoireachta na hÉireann'?

14. What does the name 'Dougal' mean in Irish?

15. What is 'uisce beatha'?

Music

answers on page 139

1. What is the real name of the lead singer in *The Commitments*?

2. Which road did The Saw Doctors sing about in a song of homesickness and emigration?

3. Which instrument is James Galway world-famous for playing?

4. What was unusual about his most famous instrument?

5. Bob Geldof co-wrote the song *Do They Know It's Christmas* with whom?

6. When did Bob Geldof's fund-raising effort Live Aid take place?

7. George Friedrich Handel was said to have used the organ in which church while composing his *Messiah*?

8. In which town was the *Londonderry Air* first noted down?

9. What is the song better known as?

10. HF Lyte, curate of Taghmon, Co. Wexford, 1815, wrote which hymn?

11. Which Irish composer wrote an opera entitled *The Intelligence Park*?

12. When and where was Gerald Barry born?

13. John McCormack, Irish singer, was famous for which singing voice?

14. Which Irish musician was once part of folk group Steeleye Span and The Pogues?

15. Who wrote the theme music for the television series *Father Ted*?

People

answers on page 140

1. Who wrote, of whom? 'fanatic, bad actress, figure of fun - She was called each.'

2. What term was used to describe the 19th century Irish gentry?

3. Which grandson of an Irish immigrant made the most famous Irish film? Name the film.

4. 'a stag's head, erased arg., charged with a trefoil slipped vert'. Which famous Irish family?

5. Who was the most famous of that particular breed?

6. What was the O'Connell motto?

7. What does this motto mean in English?

8. What is the Latin motto of the Baron O'Neill?

9. What does this motto mean in English?

10. What was J.B. Dunlop's occupation?

11. Why was James Ussher famous?

12. By which noble title was William Parsons known?

13. What is Inis mac Nesain?

14. Who called himself 'Duke of Ireland'?

15. Which famous sailor began an extensive survey of Dublin waters in December 1800?

Personalities

answers on page 140

1. George Bernard Shaw was awarded the Nobel Prize for Literature. How was his work described?

2. Giorgio and Lucia were the first-born of which Irish writer?

3. What was their mother's name?

4. Who landed at Derry on 20 May 1932, the first woman to fly across the Atlantic?

5. Charles Stewart Parnell was named as co-respondent in the divorce of which couple?

6. Which Dublin-born British admiral received the surrender of the Italian fleet in September 1943?

7. What was Henry Joy McCracken's original calling?

8. Who founded the newspaper *The United Irishman*?

9. Who was the first person charged under the Treason-Felony Act of 1848?

10. What was the first name of O'Donovan Rossa?

11. What is the real name of the 'Colleen Bawn'?

12. What was Lady Wilde also known as?

13. What was notable about John Boland in 1896?

14. Who was the 'fair-haired wonder from Cahirciveen'?

15. What is Maureen Fitzsimons famous for?

Poetry

answers on page 140

1. In which northern county was Nobel Poetry Laureate Seamus Heaney born?

2. Which Irish poet was awarded the Nobel Prize in 1923?

3. The Aeir, or Satire of the Bards, was capable of what feat?

4. When did WB Yeats die?

5. Who wrote the poem *The Lark in the Clear Air*?

6. Who wrote *The Croppy Boy*?

7. Who wrote the poem *The Famine Year*?

8. Who wrote 'We are wretches, famished, scorned, human tools to build your pride'?

9. Who wrote the poem *I am Ireland*?

10. Which Irish poet died in Flanders 31st July 1917?

11. Which poet wrote the first manifesto of the United Irishmen?

12. What were Oliver Goldsmith's last words, in reply to the enquiry 'Is your mind at ease?'

13. Which poet wrote 'Ireland is hooey'?

14. Which poet wrote *Stella's Birthday*?

15. Who was the subject of Eileen O'Leary's poem entitled *The Lament for...* ?

Specials

answers on page 140

1. Kissing the Stone in Blarney Castle is said to confer which talent?

2. What are the Stags of Broad Haven?

3. What is The Rower?

4. Rathlin island has how many lighthouses?

5. Who wrote 'Am I a free man in England, and do I become a slave in six hours by crossing the Channel'?

6. Which Irish province sounds like a German state?

7. Why did James Joyce not protest against Japan's attack on Pearl Harbor, December 7th 1941?

8. What was a 'gallowglass'?

9. What were crannogs?

10. A statue in the GPO commemorating the 1916 Rising takes as its model which mythical figure?

11. What was Ireland's first University?

12. What were 'Hedge Schools' in the 18th century ?

13. O'Connell was buried in Glasnevin cemetery in Dublin, without which organ?

14. What is a 'donnybrook'?

15. What is the origin of 'donnybrook'?

Literature

answers on page 141

1. What is the oldest surviving manuscript written completely in the Irish language?

2. How many books did St Colmcille write in his own hand?

3. Which Irish royal acropolis was used as the name of Scarlett O'Hara's home?

4. Who wrote *Leabhar Gabhalla*?

5. Who wrote the *Book of Invasions*?

6. Where did Leopold Bloom, of *Ulysses* fame, live?

7. What was the full name of Joyce Carey, novelist?

8. What was the title of Samuel Beckett's first novel?

9. Who wrote the collection of short stories entitled *The Ballroom of Romance*?

10. When was author William Trevor Cox born?

11. Who wrote *At Swim Two Birds*?

12. Who wrote *Some Experiences of an Irish RM*?

13. What was Somerville Ross' first name?

14. Who wrote *The Life Story of Eamon de Valera*?

15. For which novel was Iris Murdoch awarded the Booker Prize?

Geography
answers on page 141

1. Where was the ancient 'Tara' brooch found?

2. Around which ancient site did Daniel O'Connell organise a his first large rally?

3. Which county of the Pale was once called 'Queen's County'?

4. What is Ireland's largest offshore island?

5. Where is Ossian buried?

6. What was unusual about Ratass, Co. Kerry?

7. What is the origin of the name Tallaght, Co. Dublin?

8. Which rock is said in folklore to be the result of demonic indigestion?

9. What is the county town of Roscommon?

10. What is the county town of Monaghan?

11. What is the county town of Sligo?

12. Which counties in the Province of Ulster are not part of Northern Ireland?

13. Where is the geographical centre of Ireland?

14. What is Ireland's second smallest county?

15. Where would you find the Jealous Wall?

History

answers on page 141

1. The quarry of Starch Hill was used as the source of stone for the construction of which Irish castle?

2. In 841, which 2 Irish ports were seized by vikings?

3. In what year were the first Viking raids on the Irish coast?

4. Brehon law operated mainly by the use of which punishment?

5. When was Brian Boru born?

6. What is the origin of the title 'Boru'?

7. Who became King of Munster in 976AD?

8. When did Brian Boru become the first High King of Ireland?

9. Which battle did Brian Boru win in 1014?

10. In which battle did Brian Boru die?

11. Which city was stormed by Strongbow before his marriage to Aoife?

12. In what year did the Plantation of Ulster begin, with the publication of *The Articles of Plantation*?

13. Which battle took place on 12th July 1691?

14. What is the Irish connection of the sole US Army survivor of Little Big Horn?

15. Who was known as the 'Father of the American Navy'?

Irish Language

answers on page 142

1. What is a 'clochán'?

2. What is 'An Chomhairle Ealaíon'?

3. What is 'Céadaoin'?

4. What is 'Déardaoin'?

5. What does 'Feabhra' mean?

6. What does 'Iúil' mean?

7. Which month in Irish is 'Samhain mean'?

8. What does the 'fainne' signify today?

9. What does 'glas' mean in Irish?

10. What would you do with 'brachán caoireola'?

11. What is 'colcannon'?

12. What is 'spideog' in English?

13. What is Ceannanus Mór in Co. Antrim?

14. What is 'Bord na Gaelige'?

15. What is the meaning of Irish word 'Corr'?

Music

answers on page 142

1. What is Van Morrison's full name?

2. In what year were The Pogues formed?

3. Sean O'Farrell is featured in which 19th century ballad?

4. What is the title of Ash's debut album?

5. Which Thin Lizzy album shares its title with a Roman Polanski film?

6. Where were the group Clannad formed?

7. Who owns Leo's?

8. Where was the writer of *The Red Flag* born?

9. Dolores O'Riordan is lead singer of which band?

10. Lord Mountcharles is connected with which high-profile Irish musical festival?

11. What is Dana's real name?

12. Who composed the music to the stage show, *Riverdance*?

13. Which Irish singer was called 'the Empress of Ireland' by Toscanini?

14. Who wrote the words to *A Soldier's Song*?

15. Which style of music was Rory Gallagher famous for?

People

answers on page 142

1. Where was 'the Irish rebel' James Connolly born?

2. What does the name 'Ossian' mean?

3. What does O'Riordan mean in Irish?

4. Who founded the Presentation Order?

5. What office did John Brinkley hold on his retirement in 1826?

6. WHD Boyle also held which title?

7. What was his nickname?

8. Which Irish saint argued that Pope Gregory's calendar was mistaken?

9. The dating of which religious festival was the subject of this disagreement?

10. Who said "righteousness without culture has a tendency to turn rancid'?

11. As what did James Larkin find notoriety?

12. Dublin's Pro-Cathedral is also known as?

13. Who conducted the *Messiah* on its first performance?

14. Who was known as Silken Thomas?

15. Which 18th-century Franciscan prior became known as the 'apostle of Newfoundland'?

Personalities

answers on page 142

1. Which Irish writer became business manager to the actor, Henry Irving?

2. Which Irish poet was a BBC producer and playwright throughout World War II?

3. How many sons did Niall of the Nine Hostages have?

4. Poet C. Day-Lewis was father to which Irish actor?

5. By what name is Maelmadoc Ua Morgair better known?

6. Who said after being sentenced to death, 'When my country takes her place among the nations of the earth, then and not until then, let my epitaph be written'?

7. Who said 'no political change whatsoever is worth the shedding of a single drop of human blood'?

8. Who challenged Daniel O'Connell to a duel in 1815?

9. Who said 'Ireland unfree shall never be at peace'?

10. How many children did Kitty O'Shea bear Charles Stewart Parnell?

11. To whom was Scrabo Tower, Newtownards, Co. Down, dedicated?

12. Who was brought to the aptly named Abbey of Swords in 1014?

13. Which Irish Antarctic explorer found the remains of Robert Falcon Scott's fatal expedition in 1911?

14. Who founded an Irish Scout movement in August 1909?

15. Who is credited with coining the phrase which became GUBU?

Poetry

answers on page 143

1. Which poet wrote *An Irish Airman Foresees His Death*?

2. In which poem does William McBurney make the following declaration?

'I bear no hate against living thing/ But I love my country above my king'

3. Who wrote the following?

'They'll say I came in Eighteen-seventy-one/ And died in ...'

4. Name the person of whom Francis Ledwidge wrote

'He shall not hear the bittern cry/ In the wild sky, where he is lain'

5. The character of Buck Mulligan in *Ulysses* is based on which poet?

6. Which of C. Day Lewis' ancestors was also a poet of renown?

7. In which poem did Samuel Beckett write 'I would like my love to die'?

8. Which poet described Belfast as 'Built on reclaimed mud'?

9. Which poem opens as follows:

'Sweet was the sound/ When oft at evening's close'?

10. Which poet wrote the poem *The Village*?

11. In which poem does the following appear:

'Could poets or could painters fix/ How angels look at thirty-six'?

12. In which language did Jonathan Swift write *Stella's Birthday*?

13. In which century was the poem or prayer *St Patrick's Breastplate* written?

14. In which language was *St Patrick's Breastplate* written?

15. When was Seamus Heaney born?

Specials   *answers on page 143*

1. What sort of animals race at Shelbourne Park Race Track?

2. Which Irish county gave its name to a famous Zorro?

3. On what date each year is 'Bloomsday' celebrated?

4. Why were defeated chiefs sometimes blinded?

5. What was 'The Pale'?

6. Who faced the death penalty or slavery in the West Indies if found east of the river Shannon after 1st May 1654?

7. What happened to the land 'freed' by this drastic declaration?

8. Why is *phytophthora infestans* feared in Ireland?

9. When was Ireland's second university formed?

10. Which Queen's colleges made up the new establishment?

11. What was the title of the university?

12. What is Rockabill?

13. Shackleton was famously ice-bound in which aptly-named ship?

14. What is unusual about the 'Electric Brae' in Co. Down?

15. Which garment would a banshee be seen washing at a stream?

Sport

answers on page 143

1. Where was Ireland's first Rugby Football Club established?

2. Ireland's first rugby international against England in 1875 fielded how many players to a side?

3. Which Irish boxing champion instructed Daniel Day-Lewis in his film portrayal of *The Boxer*?

4. Where was the world's first 'steeplechase' run?

5. Why was the 'steeplechase' so termed?

6. Who won 1886 Senior Hurling Championship?

7. When was the first RDS Horse Show?

8. Who was known as the Prince of Hurling?

9. Which two players with the same surname ended their international careers against the same side, seven years apart?

10. For which English football team did Liam Brady most famously play?

11. Which sport held a Compromise Rules Series with Gaelic football?

12. Which sport was demonstrated by Ireland and Germany in 1908 Olympics?

13. Where is the Hogan Stand?

14. By what margin did Munster defeat the All Blacks 31st October 1978?

15. Of which sport was Rinty Monaghan a famous practitioner?

Politics

answers on page 144

1. Kitty O'Shea's husband was once MP for which Irish constituency?

2. Who first used the phrase 'Ulster will fight: Ulster will be right'?

3. When was Clan na Poblachta formed?

4. When was Erskine Childers elected President of Ireland?

5. When did Erskine Childers, President of Ireland die?

6. Who was Ireland's second President?

7. For which international organisation of states does Ireland provide armed forces?

8. How long is a Presidential term?

9. Who stood for election in 1828 as 'Man of the People'?

10. Which Prime Minister of New Zealand, born in Co. Derry 1856, almost shared his name with a tractor?

11. Where did Dail Éireann first assemble?

12. When did Dail Éireann first assemble?

13. Which post did James Chicester-Clarke hold?

14. Who wrote "to my beloved son, John Redmond"?

15. Which political party did William Joyce co-found in England?

Geography

answers on page 144

1. In which county is Blarney Castle?

2. How many counties are there in Ireland?

3. Where is Kiltartan's Cross, the area mentioned in the poem *An Irish Airman Foresees His Death*?

4. From where did the 'Flight of the Earls' take place?

5. What is the closest country to the island of Ireland?

6. How many Provinces are there in present day Ireland?

7. What was the capital of the ancient Province of South Leinster?

8. Which county did Coleraine become?

9. What height is Slieve Donard?

10. Where is Carolan buried?

11. Where do the rivers Barrow and Nore rise?

12. What are Ireland's 3 highest mountains?

13. On which island in Lough Derg is St. Patrick's Purgatory?

14. What is the county town of Leitrim?

15. Where was Barry McGuigan born?

History

answers on page 144

1. Sir Arthur Wellesley, soldier and statesman, was also known as?

2. When did the 'Flight of the Earls' take place?

3. Pope Alexander III gave Henry II which title?

4. When did Oliver Cromwell land in Ireland?

5. When were Derry's gates most famously closed?

6. How many Apprentice Boys shut Derry's gates?

7. When was the Siege of Derry lifted?

8. How did Patrick Sarsfield, created Earl of Lucan in 1691, die?

9. What were the '£10' castles?

10. How far behind was DMT (Dublin Mean Time) from (GMT)?

11. What were the dimensions of the £10 castles?

12. How long did the 'Siege of Derry' last?

13. Which navies fought a battle off Castletownshend, Cork in 1602?

14. Who became Earl of Ulster in 1205?

15. Name the first turbine-engined vessel to cross the Atlantic.

People

answers on page 144

1. Irish President Mary McAleese was a Professor in which University prior to her election?

2. After whom is this establishment named?

3. Where was Irish dancing superstar Michael Flatley born?

4. What was the name of the chieftain who brought St Patrick to Slemish?

5. Who was the first and last Lord Esmonde?

6. Daniel O'Connell once refused to take an oath: his famous reason?

7. What was the origin of Wexford's Bargy dialect?

8. What is Michelle Smith's married name?

9. When was Edmund Burke born?

10. Who founded the Order, Sisters of Mercy?

11. To which Irish saint was a holy well near Liscannor, Co. Clare, dedicated?

12. Which Irish family had as its crest both 'a lion... resting the... forepaw upon... roses' and 'a wolf rampant'?

13. Who was the Marquis de St Ruth?

14. Which rugby personality's biography was self-described as "20 per cent... about rugby... 80 per cent is pornography"?

15. Who was the first archbishop of Dublin in 1162?

Specials

answers on page 145

1. What was the usual form of punishment for a chief defeated in battle?

2. Buried in Killimer, Co. Clare, how did the 'Colleen Bawn' die?

3. What gave Bloody Foreland in Donegal its name?

4. What are the Knockmealdowns?

5. What separates the gaelic and gaelic languages?

6. Which goddess was claimed by the Tuatha de Danaan?

7. Who is Ireland's 'King Arthur'?

8. What was hunted on St Stephen's Day?

9. What were 'Cornys'?

10. In the 1840s and 50s, who or what were termed 'the Pope's Brass Band'?

11. How is Lennox Robinson remembered?

12. Which Robert E. Howard character should not be depicted with long hair, and why?

13. What is The Lios?

14. Which organisation did Richard Martin help found?

15. The 'discoverer' of the potato, Sir Walter Raleigh, introduced which other famous plant to Europe?

Sport

answers on page 145

1. Which organisation owns Lansdowne Road stadium in Dublin?

2. Who was the first Irishman to win the Wimbledon tennis championship?

3. When did international showjumping begin at RDS (Ballsbridge)?

4. For which English football teams did David O'Leary play?

5. In which Olympics was John McNally a winner?

6. In which Olympics did Ireland gain a bantamweight Bronze medal?

7. In which year did Frederick Gilroy win Olympic Bronze?

8. At which weights did Frederick Gilroy and Anthony Byrne win Bronze medals?

9. Frederick Tiedt won which Olympic boxing Silver medal?

10. Which Olympic events did John Boland win in 1896?

11. Which Formula One motor-racing team features Eddie Irvine?

12. Which sport which originated in Ireland is also an offence in soccer?

13. St. George McCarthy was a founder member of the GAA, and a member of which other organisation?

14. What distinction does sportsman Kevin Moran hold?

15. How many times did he receive this distinction?

Politics

answers on page 145

1. Edward Carson was first elected to Parliament for which constituency?

2. Who founded Fenian Brotherhood secret society?

3. Who founded the Progressive Democrats?

4. How many Presidents has Ireland had up until 2000?

5. To what was the Ulster Solemn League and Covenant in 1912 in opposition?

6. What was the duration of the first Northern Ireland Assembly?

7. Which political party did de Valera form in 1926?

8. What does 'Fianna Fail' mean in English?

9. Who introduced the first Irish Home Rule Bill?

10. Which President was elected by the largest margin?

11. Which 2 constituencies were held by Eoin MacNeill in first Dail?

12. What is the English translation of Fine Gael?

13. Who was the first leader of the SDLP?

14. Who formed Fianna Fail?

15. What was Taoiseach Jack Lynch's less well-known second name?

Geography

answers on page 146

1. Where is Port Erin?

2. Where was George Stokes, physicist, born?

3. What is the main industry of Donegal's Killybegs?

4. Where is the Irish Equine Centre?

5. Where does James Galway now reside?

6. What does Waterville, Co. Kerry's Irish name, 'An Coireán' mean?

7. Dun Laoghaire was once called?

8. Where was Charles Stewart Parnell born?

9. Where was St. Brendan born?

10. What is the 4th highest Irish mountain?

11. In which county is Lough Kee?

12. In which county was Peter O'Toole born?

13. In which county was artist Roderic O'Connor in 1860 born?

14. The Ardigeen River flows through which county?

15. In which county is the country house Heywood?

History

answers on page 146

1. Who landed 1,000 men at Killala, Co. Mayo in 1798?

2. Which organisations fought the 'Battle of the Diamond'?

3. What is the origin of Swords, Co. Dublin?

4. In which year did St Patrick's Day become a Bank Holiday?

5. What name was Patrick Sarsfield given on being knighted?

6. In 1446, what marked 'an Irish enemy'?

7. What arrived in Ireland in 1348?

8. How did Strongbow die, according to the Four Masters?

9. At the time of Queen Elizabeth I, where was 'the most perilous place in all the isle'?

10. What did French General Humbert establish in Ireland in 1798?

11. Where was the first 'Irish Republic'?

12. Who was the President of Humbert's 'Republic'?

13. In 1798, who was the Knight of Kerry?

14. When and where was 'Lord Haw-Haw' executed?

15. Which Irish writer wrote scripts for Lord Haw-Haw?

Irish Language

answers on page 146

1. What is 'Mhairt'?

2. What is 'Aoine'?

3. What does 'Éanair' mean?

4. What does 'Márta' mean?

5. The Irish language symbol of a left to right diagonal is called?

6. What is gaelic football in Irish?

7. What is a 'sliotar'?

8. What does TD stand for?

9. What is Dail Éireann?

10. What was a 'seanachie'?

11. What does 'ban' mean in Irish?

12. What is Bord Fáilte?

13. What was an 'aenach'?

14. What does 'saoirse' mean?

15. What was 'caid'?

Music

answers on page 146

1. Which two instruments does Van Morrison usually play?

2. Dave Fanning is a famous DJ on which Irish radio station?

3. For which charity organisation was *Feed the World* the theme song?

4. What is the full 'title' of Bono, from U2?

5. What is the origin of this 'title'?

6. In the song, exactly how many 'shades of green' can be found in Ireland?

7. Who composed the music to the *Star-Spangled Banner*?

8. The Pogues and Kirsty MacColl sang of *Fairytale of...*?

9. What is the origin of the band title 'The Pogues'?

10. Who was lead singer of The Pogues in the 1980s?

11. Percy French wrote about which Eastern figure?

12. Who wrote the opera *Duenna*?

13. What is the real name of U2's 'Bono'?

14. What band of a similar name did Shane MacGowan (ex-Pogues) form?

15. What is Chris de Burgh's real name?

People

answers on page 147

1. What was the nickname of snooker champion Alex Higgins?

2. Wolfe Tone is a famous of the eighteenth-century figure.. What was his first name?

3. Who was the Red Earl of Ulster?

4. Which religious order was founded by Edmund Burke's mother?

5. A Gore-Booth motto runs 'quod ero spero'. What does this Latin phrase mean?

6. In 1861, Irish people made up what percentage of the population of Western Australia?

7. When did Lady Morgan die?

8. Who said "We are fighting for bread and butter"?

9. Who said that sex "never came to Ireland until Teilifis Éireann went on the air"?

10. To whom was he speaking?

11. What is 'Mo' short for in 'Mo' Mowlam?

12. What was Grace O'Malley's feared title?

13. Who was the architect of Dublin's General Post Office?

14. Who began the successful east-west flight across the Atlantic from Ireland?

15. Bernardo O'Higgins is known as?

Poetry

answers on page 147

1. By what other name is *St Patrick's Breastplate* known?

2. What is Seamus Heaney's full name?

3. Who wrote the poem Ulster 1912?

4. Who wrote the epic satirical poem *The Midnight Court*?

5. Which Irish writer penned a poem entitled *Universal Beauty*?

6. In which poem does WB Yeats write 'my countrymen Kiltartan's poor'?

7. Who wrote The *Fiddler of Dooney*?

8. Of what materials was Yeats' 'small cabin' constructed?

9. Which Yeats' poem provided the lyrics for a popular song?

10. Who wrote 'Romantic Ireland's dead and gone'?

11. Which cleric-poet was once Professor of Greek at University College Dublin?

12. 'Father Prout' was the pen-name of?

13. John O'Leary, Fenian, is immortalised by Yeats in which poem?

14. Which poet is reputed to have written part of his *Faerie Queen* at Lismore Castle?

15. In which language did Brian Merriman write *The Midnight Court*?

Specials

answers on page 147

1. In which year was 'Bloomsday' first celebrated with a week of celebration?

2. Why is 'Bloomsday' so-called?

3. After whom were the 4th century Irish Fenian warriors named?

4. What are 'Mass Rocks'?

5. What is another name for the Great Skellig?

6. What does GUBU stand for?

7. Where would you find 'Seven Heads'?

8. Which Kilkenny great house, burned down in 1922, shares its name with the greatest American festival of the 1960s?

9. Why was part of Carlow Castle demolished in the 1880s?

10. What is the unit of currency in Ireland?

11. Who or what was 'Roaring Meg'?

12. What is Ireland's Eye?

13. What is Dundrod, Co. Antrim, famous for?

14. According to the song, to what should you 'treat your Mary-Anne'?

15. Where might you find 'Finn MacCool's Fingers'?

Sport

answers on page 148

1. Which rugby clubs play at Lansdowne Road?

2. Where was Willie John McBride born?

3. Which northern Rugby legend led the British Lions in 1974?

4. For which English football teams did Frank Stapleton play?

5. Which sport does Darren Clarke play?

6. Padraig Harrington missed out on a golf championship in 2000 for what unusual reason?

7. Who won his first Grand National in 2000?

8. Which Irish-trained horse did Ruby Walsh ride to Grand National victory?

9. Who trained the 153rd Grand National winner in 2000?

10. What is the connection between trainer and rider of Papillon?

11. What is the connection between winning horses in 1999-2000 Grand National races?

12. What is unusual about the winner and runner-up in the 1998 Irish Grand National?

13. David O'Leary manages which soccer team?

14. Which horse won the Grand National in 1998?

15. In which sport was John J. Flanagan (1873-1938) famous?

Politics

answers on page 148

1. Which Irishman became President of Israel?

2. When was the Progressive Democrat party formed in Ireland?

3. Where was Douglas Hyde, future Irish President, born?

4. How many female Presidents has Ireland had up until 2000?

5. What was notable about the Ulster Solemn League and Covenant in 1912?

6. Which Irish President could be described as Hispano-Celtic?

7. What is the minimum age of an Irish president?

8. How many times was Charles Haughey Irish Prime Minister?

9. Who did Mary McAleese 'defeat' in the Presidential election?

10. What is the English translation of Fianna Fail?

11. What was "the best machine... for governing a country against its will"?

12. Who said this "...whatever happens, my own countrymen won't kill me"?

13. When did Michael Collins die?

14. Who described de Valera as a "Spanish onion"?

15. Which party does David Trimble lead?

Literature

1. From which myth cycle was *The Cattle Raid* ᴏ̣

2. In what language was the *Book of Kells* written?

3. Who wrote *The Quare Fellow*?

4. Sheridan le Fanu's *Carmilla* is a variation on which monster?

5. In which year is *Ulysses* set?

6. Who wrote *A Modest Proposal*?

7. Which satirical novel sounds like a wildlife documentary?

8. Who was the first Irish winner of the Booker Prize?

9. Who wrote an *Argument against abolishing Christianity*?

10. To which 'Hidden Ireland' did Daniel Corkery refer?

11. What is the name of the estate in Colleen McCullough's *Thorn Birds*?

12. Which Dublin town is the setting for Sheridan le Fanu's *The House By The Churchyard*?

13. Which American writer of the *Pern* novels now lives in Ireland?

14. Brian O'Nolan is the real name of which Irish author?

15. What was Martin Ross' real name?

...ot Press magazine deals with which industry?

2. What entertainment did James Joyce and partners provide from December 20th 1909?

3. How long did the first steam ship take to cross of the Atlantic ?

4. Which shorthand inventor was born in Rockcorry, Co. Monaghan?

5. In which industry was Sion Mills in Tyrone involved?

6. What product is produced by a company headquartered at Tandragee Castle?

7. Who was reputed to be the owner of Ireland's first petrol-driven motor car?

8. What was the Nobel 2000?

9. Who developed the pneumatic tyre?

10. What was constructed by shipbuilders Malcomson of Waterford?

11. What was this vessel called?

12. Which sister ship of *Titanic* had an equally 'striking' history?

13. What did Belfast's Hickson's shipyard become in 1861?

14. In 1911, what were the three largest ships in the world?

15. What tonnage was each of the vessels?

Films

answers on page 149

1. Which Alan Parker film featured a group of Dublin teenagers forming a band?

2. Which film featured Bronagh Gallagher alongside Eric Stoltz and John Travolta?

3. Bronagh Gallagher featured in which film where she carried Liam Neeson?

4. Which film featured Liam Neeson as a character with a 'dark' side?

5. Which film featured the lead singer of the Irish band The Corrs, as well as Madonna?

6. Which film features Ewan McGregor as an Irish novelist?

7. Which two films (that aren't *Rob Roy*) prominently feature Liam Neeson fighting with swords?

8. Which film famously features Van Morrison singing *Moondance*?

9. Where was the film *Excalibur* principally filmed?

10. Brendan Gleeson appeared in which film as a police inspector on the trail of two Dublin runaways?

11. Gabriel Byrne appears as a master criminal in which film?

12. Which two films of 1999 starred Gabriel Byrne on either side of good and evil?

13. In which film did Brendan Gleeson appear alongside Mel Gibson, not as an Irishman, but a Scot?

14. Cyril Cusack starred in Francois Truffaut's film of which Ray Bradbury story?

15. Which Irish actress played Jane to Johnny Weissmuller's *Tarzan* in the 1940s?

Geography

answers on page 149

1. In which Irish city was the television series *Tolka Row* set?

2. Where did Robert the Bruce take refuge after his defeat, and learn to 'try and try again' from the spider in his cave?

3. Which river flows through Belfast?

4. What is the closest country to the Republic of Ireland, politically?

5. Which county is associated with the Errigal mountains?

6. How many Provinces were there in medieval times?

7. What was the capital of the ancient Province of North Leinster?

8. Where is Slemish mountain?

9. Where was the Fenian Brotherhood founded?

10. Name 3 Glens of Antrim?

11. Which Tipperary hills once contained coal deposits?

12. Where was Sir Hans Sloane born?

13. What was the former name of Randalstown, Co. Antrim?

14. What is the origin of the name Tara, Co. Meath?

15. Where was Catherine, 2nd wife of 12th Earl of Desmond born?

History

answers on page 149

1. How did Wolfe Tone die?

2. What is unusual about Ireland's Nobel Peace awards?

3. Two men of which name suffered opposite fates 'for Ireland'?

4. Which medal was awarded to the RUC in April 2000?

5. What was the name of the first US-commissioned warship, which John Barry captained?

6. Who landed in Dingle Bay in 1579, leading a Munster rebellion?

7. Who financed many of the soldiers taking part in the expedition?

8. What date was the Easter Rising?

9. Who stole the Crown Jewels from the Tower of London in May 1671?

10. Who, after his death, was described as "the destroyer of Ireland in general"?

11. The 5th Earl of Donegall owned land around which area in late 1760s?

12. When was the RIC disbanded?

13. When was Ireland's first department store opened?

14. When was the first electric tramway in the British Isles opened?

15. Who is the famous partner of William Hare?

Irish Language

answers on page 150

1. What is 'Domnach'?

2. What does 'Aibréan' mean?

3. What does 'Mean Fómhair' mean?

4. What is 'Mí na Nollaig'?

5. What is 'hurling' in Irish?

6. What is a 'camán'?

7. What is 'Seanad Éireann'?

8. What does 'gorm' mean in Irish?

9. What were the 'sidhe'?

10. Who or what is De Danaan?

11. What was Teampall Mór?

12. What does the slogan 'Erin Go Bragh' mean?

13. What is Irish for 'deer'?

14. What is the 'shanvanvocht'?

15. What is 'horse' in Irish?

Music

answers on page 150

1. Neil Hannon, of the 'Divine Comedy', takes his name from which Italian poet's work?

2. *The Ballad of Owen Roe* concerns which Irish noble?

3. Which poet wrote the unofficial Irish anthem *A Nation Once Again*?

4. When did The Rolling Stones first play in Ireland?

5. What do the Mourne Mountains famously do, according to Percy French's song?

6. Name the members of U2?

7. Which member of U2 is not Irish?

8. Which Irish groups feature members of the Lynch family?

9. Which boy band achieved a record 5 No.1s with their first 5 singles?

10. By what other name is Sinead O'Connor now to be known?

11. Who is the singer songwriter brother of Irish singer-songwriter Luka Bloom?

12. Which ballad contains the line "For the sake of my religion I was forced to leave my native home"?

13. Which song of *Father Ted*'s Dougal was written by Neil 'Divine Comedy' Hannon?

14. Which Irish singer-songwriter is most famous for *Lady in Red*?

15. Where was flautist James Galway born?

People

answers on page 150

1. Which Irishman won the Nobel Peace Prize in 1974?

2. What was the calling of Donagh, son of Thomas McDonagh?

3. What was Hugh O'Neill also known as?

4. On which infamous murder did Gerald Griffin base *The Collegians*?

5. What do the Dunlop brothers owe to a famous Belfast vet?

6. What is the significance of Harriet Shaw Weaver to Irish literature?

7. In 1847 who was described as 'a feeble old man muttering from a table'?

8. Who was awarded Nobel Prize with Sinton, 1951?

9. Who was Michael Collins' fiancée?

10. Where was Harry Ferguson born?

11. Who formed the Brothers of the Christian Schools (Christian Brothers)?

12. For which church was Richard Whately Archbishop of Dublin?

13. Who was Ellen Bischoffsheim?

14. Which business was the Countess of Desart responsible for?

15. What is the name of Dave Perry's computer software company?

Personalities

answers on page 150

1. Which Irish-born author died the same day as President Kennedy and Aldous Huxley?

2. What was 'Napper' Tandy's first name?

3. Who was born in Nobber, Co. Meath, in 1670?

4. What age was Catherine, 2nd wife of 12th Earl of Desmond said to have reached?

5. Where was Tom Crean born?

6. Which Irishman was the first European to sight Antarctica, 1819?

7. WHD Boyle, related to scientist Robert Boyle, held which military post?

8. James Charles O'Connor from Cork was famous for promoting which language?

9. What was Cuchulainn's original name?

10. Who was an astronomer of note and a successful fish farmer?

11. Which Irish physicist was awarded the Nobel Prize in 1951?

12. Which post did George Stokes hold in common with Sir Joseph Larmor?

13. When was Brian Merriman born?

14. Which Irish figurehead wrote 'Romantic Ireland's dead and gone/ It's with O'Leary in the grave'?

15. Who is described in this verse? 'a haggard woman returned and Dublin went wild to meet her'.

Religion

answers on page 151

1. Lough Derg is a pilgrimage site for which Saint?

2. Who was once known as the 'first Patrick'?

3. St. Brendan most commonly referred to as?

4. Which Roman Catholic cleric was archbishop of Melbourne, Australia for 45 years until his death in 1963?

5. The Cross of Cong, fashioned c.1125 in Roscommon, was made to house which relic?

6. Which Co. Cavan bishop first translated the Bible into Irish?

7. Which medieval order once maintained a base in Ross Carbery, Co. Cork?

8. Which Pope first forbade the pilgrimages to St. Patrick's Purgatory?

9. Which saint was said to have cursed Tara?

10. Tara was damaged in the 19th century in a fruitless search for which religious artefact?

11. When is the feast day of St Brendan?

12. Complete the 17th century phrase 'If there were no priests, there would be no...'?

13. When did St. Fergal die?

14. When was Kilcooly Abbey founded?

15. When was the *Messiah* first performed?

Specials

answers on page 151

1. What, after potatoes, is the main ingredient of champ?

2. What is Irish Mist?

3. What is 'a wake'?

4. What status did UNESCO confer on the Giant's Causeway?

5. How much larger is the monument at Newgrange than that of Knowth?

6. Where would you find the Bull, Heifer and Cow?

7. To which post was Mrs Mary Westby appointed in 1760?

8. What was Haulbowline?

9. What was a 'nickey'?

10. What first appeared in public on Kingstown's East Pier in 1852?

11. What is unusual about the 1920s yacht Saoirse?

12. Which Irish lawyer is connected to the theatre by a playwright and a postal order?

13. Why might this person be so described?

14. What was created in Doohulla, Connemara in 1854?

15. What is notable about Dublin's Rotunda hospital?

Sport

answers on page 151

1. In which event did Ronnie Bennett win Olympic gold?

2. When did Michelle Smith win Olympic swimming gold?

3. Which Irish international shares his name with an English snooker player?

4. For which English football teams did Pat Jennings play?

5. How many boxing medals did Ireland win in the 1952 Olympics?

6. Who trained and rode Bobbyjo?

7. What distinction does trainer Ted Walsh hold as a jockey?

8. Which 'Grand' horserace did Jonjo O'Neill never win?

9. In which sport do Neil Booth and Jeremy Henry represent Ireland?

10. Darren Clarke won World Match Play in 2000 by beating which golfer?

11. For which American soccer side did George Best play for in 1976?

12. Tony McCoy set which world record in the 1997-8 season?

13. Which Dublin golf course was designed by Christy O'Connor?

14. Trinity College, Dublin's rugby club holds which distinction?

15. When was Trinity's rugby club officially founded?

Television

answers on page 152

1. When was RTÉ established?

2. From which transmitter did regular TV broadcasting start in Ireland?

3. On which Irish TV show did Boyzone first appear?

4. Who hosted *The Late Late Show* for the longest period?

5. Who now hosts *The Late Late Show*?

6. Which long-running game-show did Irish comedian Roy Walker present?

7. Roy Walker's famous catchphrase from *Catchphrase* was?

8. What are the 2 most famous aliens on Irish TV?

9. What kind of animal is Dustin?

10. Where was the series *Ballykissangel* filmed?

11. What was the name of the public house in *Ballykissangel*?

12. What was the name of the character played by Dervla Kirwan?

13. What is Dustin's occupation?

14. Which Irish media personality has covered Eurovision Song Contest for both RTÉ and BBC?

15. In which year did *The Late Late Show* begin?

Natural History

answers on page 152

1. Which Irish university has its own zoo?

2. Who introduced the word 'electron'?

3. Which theory of William Rowan Hamilton is important in quantum physics?

4. William Rowan Hamilton held which post at the age of 22?

5. Which mathematician died in Ireland 8th December, 1864, having taught there for many years?

6. What is another name for 'dulse'?

7. Which Irish cleric is noted for his mathematical prowess?

8. Who was known as 'the father of American chemistry'?

9. What was the maximum magnification of the 'Leviathan'?

10. Which scientific post was held by the 3rd Earl of Rosse hold 1848-54?

11. What is the son of 3rd Earl of Rosse best remembered for?

12. Why might 1st Earl of Cork & Orrery be described as 'the grandfather of chemistry'?

13. Who was the first Astronomer Royal for Ireland?

14. Which Irish scientist mapped the earth's magnetic field?

15. When were Dublin's first zoological gardens opened?

History

answers on page 152

1. What did Daniel O'Connell once call Sir Robert Peel?

2. When did Bernadette Devlin make her House of Commons 'maiden speech'?

3. Which party did Garret Fitzgerald lead?

4. When did former Irish President Douglas Hyde die?

5. Which UN Commission had ex-President Mary Robinson as its head?

6. Who was Prime Minister of Northern Ireland, 1921-40?

7. Who founded Sinn Féin?

8. Who described O'Connell as 'a feeble old man'?

9. When was the first Irish Home Rule Bill introduced?

10. Who was to represent Co. Armagh in the first Dail?

11. Where was Chaim Herzog born?

12. Which party does John Hume lead?

13. What does UUP stand for?

14. Who founded the Home Government Association in 1870?

15. Who was the first Cork man to become Taoiseach?

Arts

answers on page 152

1. Which English magazine first serialised James Joyce's novel, *A Portrait of the Artist as a Young Man* in 1914?

2. Which songwriter and artist wrote *The Mountains of Mourne*?

3. When was payment for bardic poems fixed?

4. Where was the other end of the 'wireless' telegraph from Ireland?

5. Which is Ireland's longest surviving newspaper?

6. What is Ireland's second oldest newspaper?

7. What is Ireland's third oldest newspaper?

8. Which award did Peter O'Toole receive from a magazine in April 2000?

9. Who wrote that 'A people without a language is only half a nation'?

10. Where was artist Francis Bacon born?

11. For which works is Francis Bacon best-remembered?

12. What was Lady Gregory's full name?

13. What is the modern name of the *West Cork Eagle and County Advertiser*?

14. What was the *West Cork Eagle*'s promotional boast?

15. Which Cork newspaper shares its name with the Antipodean counterpart of Polaris?

Geography

answers on page 153

1. There were three further Queen's colleges or universities founded in Ireland in the nineteenth century. Where are they?

2. Which County Mayo town featured in John Ford's *The Quiet Man*?

3. How many glens are there in the world-famous 'Glens of Antrim'?

4. Of which Irish cities was President John F Kennedy given the 'Freedom' on his visit to Ireland in 1963?

5. What is the closest country to the Republic of Ireland, physically?

6. Which of the present-day Provinces is comprised of two of the ancient Provinces?

7. Domangard, 5th century bishop and founder of Maghera, County Derry, gave his name to which mountain?

8. Which county is famous for its Nine Glens?

9. Name another 3 Glens of Antrim?

10. The Druid's Seat and Glendruid House may be found near which area of Co. Dublin?

11. Off which part of the Irish coastline was the American liner *Lusitania* torpedoed by German submarine in 1915?

12. What river flowed through Randalstown?

13. What is the county town of Mayo?

14. What is the county town of Longford?

15. What is the county town of Carlow?

History

answers on page 153

1. When was the Bank of Ireland founded?

2. Who said of Kinsale in 1601 'I hold this town for Christ and the King of Spain'?

3. Who announced the American Declaration of Independence?

4. Which Irish division fought and lost 5,000 men at the Battle of the Somme?

5. What happened to the two Erskine Childers'?

6. What became of Padraig Pearse's former schoolhouse?

7. Where was the Dublin terminus of the Great Northern Railway?

8. Who was crowned King of Ireland in 1316?

9. When were the 'peelers' formed?

10. When did Henry Grattan make his 'Declaration of Rights'?

11. What was 'Saorstát Éireann'?

12. Who said 'You can't switch on peace like a light'?

13. When was the electric tramway between Portrush and Bushmills finally closed?

14. When was the University of Ulster established?

15. When was the garden at Heywood designed?

Music

answers on page 153

1. Which European city gave guitarist Gary Moore his biggest hit?

2. Where did ex-Beautiful South singer Brianna Corrigan come from?

3. Who wrote the words to the song *My Lagan Love*?

4. According to the song, where was *The Sash* worn?

5. What is the real name of U2's 'The Edge'?

6. Which Prince song gave Sinead O'Connor her first world wide hit?

7. What is Luka Bloom's real name?

8. Which Irish tenor was the subject of the film *Hear My Song*?

9. Who was the 'Wild Colonial Boy' of the song?

10. Where was Jack Donohue born?

11. Chris de Burgh wrote which extra-terrestrial themed Christmas song?

12. What was the original title of the Irish 'boy-band' Westlife?

13. What was the title of Dana's entry in the Eurovision Song Contest?

14. Who wrote *The Bells of Shandon*?

15. Which group features Paddy Moloney and Derek Bell?

People

answers on page 154

1. To whom does the film title *Nora* refer?

2. Sean MacBride, joint winner of the 1974 Nobel Peace Prize, was son to which famous Irish nationalist and literary inspiration?

3. Who was Sweeney Menn?

4. Which Irishman and Canadian Minister for Agriculture was assassinated?

5. What is John Philip Holland credited with?

6. Who was 'Sir' Dan Donnelly?

7. Who was 'Devil Dill'?

8. What nationality was Robert Flaherty, documentary film-maker?

9. Who termed the Aran Islands "Three stepping stones out of Europe"?

10. Which Irish naval officer received the German Naval surrender at Scapa Flow in 1919?

11. For which first was James Dixon responsible in 1803?

12. Charles David Lucas received a medal on 26th June 1857. What was it?

13. How has the Irish name Aoife been anglicised?

14. Who began construction of Carrickfergus castle?

15. What was boxer Dave McAuley's nickname?

Specials

answers on page 154

1. What were 'Suffolk Fencibles' and 'Ancient Britons'?

2. What was described as 'this noble weapon glittering above us'?

3. What is *Chondrus crispus*?

4. What was the 'Leviathan of Parsonstown'?

5. What was first set on a Dublin sandbar in 1735?

6. Why is Pigeon House so-called?

7. What was a 'Galway hooker'?

8. Who was 'A Silent Politician'?

9. According to Royal Navy Admiral Domville, who was 'a quiet little man with the courage of a lion'?

10. What reason would Admiral Domville have for this description?

11. What may be found between Twelve Pins and Ballyconneely Bay?

12. What are Barrcostello, Emlaghmore and Barrowen?

13. What, originally, was 'kelp'?

14. What icon did Cedric Gibbons design?

15. What is 'fives'?

Sport

answers on page 154

1. In which Olympic Games did Ronnie Bennett win Olympic gold?

2. How many medals was Michelle Smith awarded in 1996?

3. With which two teams did the 1972 All Blacks touring side draw in Ireland?

4. Which team won the 1972 Five Nations?

5. Which Irish soccer international began and ended his career against Belgium in the 1920s and 30s?

6. Which footballer played in only one international, in the World Cup campaign of 1937?

7. Who was termed the "'Babe Ruth' of Gaelic football" in 1947?

8. How many boxing medals did Ireland win in the 1932 Olympics?

9. How many Olympic yachting medals has Ireland won?

10. How many official horse racecourses are there in Ireland?

11. Which rugby club rather aptly won the first three years of the Senior Cup?

12. What is noteworthy about the 1922 Ulster Grand Prix?

13. Who won the first Ulster Grand Prix?

14. Which vehicle competed in the Ulster Grand Prix?

15. How many Olympic golds did John J. Flanagan win in his career?

Politics

answers on page 154

1. When did Charles Haughey become Taoiseach?

2. Which title did James Craig take on being knighted?

3. Who was the first president of the Irish Free State?

4. Which party does Monica McWilliams lead?

5. Which American office did Thomas Emmet, United Irishman, hold?

6. When was the SDLP formed?

7. Whose election address was given as '143 Leinster Road, Rathmines, Co. Dublin'?

8. The ILPU changed its name to what in the 1920s?

9. Which politicians jointly won the Nobel Peace Prize in 1999?

10. What does SDLP stand for?

11. Which party does Rev. Ian Paisley lead?

12. Which election saw the first Fianna Fail election contest?

13. On putting his name to the Anglo-Irish Treaty of 1921, who said 'I have signed my own death warrant'?

14. Which constituency has been represented for many years by Rev. Ian Paisley?

15. Which Roscommon priest was once vice-chairman of Sinn Fein?

Literature

answers on page 155

1. Which novelist wrote the book on which the film *The Snapper* is based?

2. Who wrote *Leaves from a Prison Diary*?

3. Which Irish writer was grant funded by Royal Literary Fund in 1915?

4. Who wrote *Soggarth Aroon* in 1831?

5. What was the subject of *Soggarth Aroon*?

6. Where was author William Trevor Cox born?

7. Whose autobiography was entitled *An Only Child*?

8. What was Somerville's first name?

9. When was *Dublin University Magazine* first published?

10. To which city according to one author does the description 'strumpet' apply?

11. Who wrote the book *Cal*?

12. Where was Lawrence Sterne born?

13. Which Irish author won the Whitbread Prize in 1988?

14. Brian O'Nolan is also the real name of which Irish author?

15. What do the *Book of Leinster* and the *Book of Armagh* contain?

Industry

answers on page 155

1. Early in 2000, Ireland was named the world's largest exporter of which commodity?

2. What percentage of Ireland's energy needs is met by nuclear energy?

3. Which type of pottery is produced in Belleek?

4. Which company popularised Ferguson's tractor?

5. What did John de Lorean set up in Co. Antrim during the 1980s?

6. What was unusual about the bodywork of a classic de Lorean car?

7. What make of car did Dr. Colohon own?

8. Which motor vehicle was produced in a Cork factory by 1917?

9. What make of tractors were produced?

10. Who produced the Nobel 2000 in Co. Down?

11. In 1921 who were 'The Only Motor Car Manufacturers in Ireland'?

12. What nationality was J.B. Dunlop, father of the pneumatic tyre?

13. When was the Belleek Pottery founded?

14. Which Wexford export was enjoyed in England from 1171?

15. Where was Ireland's first aeroplane flown?

Films

answers on page 155

1. John Boorman directed Brendan Gleeson in which film based on the life of a 'colourful' Dublin criminal?

2. What was unusual about this 1998 film?

3. Which Irish band of the 1960s takes its name from a 1950s American science fiction film about giant ants?

4. James Mason, as a weary member of 'the organisation', is wounded in a botched robbery in which Carol Reed film?

5. Victor McLaglen appeared in an earlier film by John Ford, from a play about the IRA. What was its title?

6. Which Irish actor appeared in the Roger Vadim film *Barbarella*, as the villainous Duran Duran?

7. Which Irish actor famously played opposite Charlton Heston in Ben Hur?

8. Stephen Boyd played opposite Raquel Welsh in which submarine drama?

9. Which films featured a De Lorean car prominently?

10. At what speed did Dr Brown's De Lorean achieve time travel?

11. Which film maker produced *Man of Aran* in 1934?

12. Neil Jordan won which Oscar for his film *The Crying Game*?

13. In which year was Benjamin George the first Irish winner of an Academy Award?

14. Greer Garson won an Oscar in 1942 for her portrayal of which courageous character?

15. What is the character played by John Wayne in *The Quiet Man*?

Geography

answers on page 156

1. What was the capital of the ancient Province of Munster?

2. Name yet another 3 Glens of Antrim?

3. What is the county town of Waterford?

4. What is the county town of Wexford?

5. What is the county town of Cavan?

6. In which city was the scientist who defined absolute zero born?

7. Through which county does the Kenmare River flow?

8. Through which city does the River Nore pass?

9. How large is Lough Neagh?

10. Where are the North and South Slobs?

11. Which area held "no water to drown a man, no timber to hang him and no soil to bury him"?

12. Where is Bully's Acre?

13. Where is Bullock?

14. Which county has an area of 4255sq km?

15. Which county has an area of 2463sq km?

History

answers on page 156

1. When did Kilkenny become a city?

2. When was a bounty of £1,000 placed on the head of Hugh O'Neill?

3. According to Lord Cornwallis what was 'the favourite pastime' of such militias as the 'Suffolk Fencible's during 1798?

4. When did King James land in Ireland, prior to the Battle of the Boyne?

5. In what year was the proclamation 'The Provisional Government to the People of Ireland'?

6. Who made the proclamation of 'The Provisional Government to the People of Ireland'?

7. When did the first of Daniel O'Connell's 'monster meetings' take place at Tara?

8. When did the Irish 'tricolour' first appear?

9. Who described the Irish tricolour as a 'noble weapon'?

10. What led to Art O'Leary's death?

11. Why should O'Leary have been expected to sell his horse for a small price?

12. When did Wolfe Tone die?

13. When was Wolfe Tone born?

14. What were 'Carders' in the early 18th century?

15. Which port suffered a blockade from 2nd May-16th October 1649?

Irish Language

answers on page 156

1. What is 'Sathairn'?

2. What does 'Meitheamh' mean?

3. What does 'Lúnasa' mean?

4. What does 'Deireamh Fómhair' mean?

5. Which Irish man's name is often confused with an English woman's name?

6. What does 'flannbhui' mean in Irish?

6. What does 'dearg' mean in Irish?

8. What are 'cruibíns'?

9. What is Bord na Mona?

10. What was An Claidheamh Soluis?

11. What is the meaning of 'banshee'?

12. What is 'observatory' in Irish?

13. What does Boa Island mean in Irish?

14. What does 'uisce beatha' mean?

15. Who or what is 'sheela-na-gig'?

Music

answers on page 156

1. Name the town which completes this song title: *Sean South of...*?

2. Where, according to the song, did Roddy McCorley die?

3. Which Irish musician was famous for her virtuosity on the harp, appearing many times on television?

4. *Eleven O'Clock Tick Tock* was an early single by which group?

5. Where did U2 first meet?

6. Of which Christian denomination did Sinead O'Connor become a priest?

7. Which Irish groups has Christy Moore played in?

8. Which Irish singer is famous for his cardigans and rocking chair?

9. Where was Chris de Burgh born?

10. For which Stanley Kubrick film did The Chieftains provide music?

11. When did The Corrs release *Forgiven Not Forgotten*?

12. Barry Douglas is a famous Irish musician. What instrument does he play?

13. Who is well-acquainted with both *Patricia the Stripper* and the *Lady in Red*?

14. With which Irish 'boy-band' did Ronan Keating come to notice?

15. When did the first Irish duo win Eurovision Song Contest for Ireland?

People

answers on page 157

1. What is the full name of WB Yeats?

2. Who wrote that 'National poetry is the very flowering of the soul'?

3. Turlough O'Carolan is more commonly known as?

4. Whose last words were 'Either the wallpaper goes or I do'?

5. What was Ireland's population in 1956?

6. Which Cavan GAA star became Tánaiste in 1993?

7. Who was Jonathan Swift's literary muse, 'Vanessa'?

8. How was General 'Tim' Pile involved in World War II?

9. In which field was Jack Yeats, brother of William Butler Yeats, a famous Irish figure?

10. Which heraldic crest is described 'coronet robin redbreast with a laurel in beak'?

11. What is the Irish motto of O'Sullivan Mór?

12. What does this motto mean in English?

13. Which heraldic crest is appears to show 'a robin redbreast on a green lizard'?

14. What did Sub Lieutenant AWS Tisdall receive during World War One?

15. Where was AWS Tisdall born?

Specials

answers on page 157

1. In what month is the Auld Lammas Fair held in Ballycastle, Co. Antrim?

2. Which article depicts 'two hands clasping a crowned heart'?

3. Which readily available type of 'food' was promoted in the satirical pamphlet *A Modest Proposal*?

4. How is Unshin better known?

5. What was Clann na Talmhan?

6. What were the 'Lays of the Western Gael'?

7. Who or what was Jammie Clinch?

8. What is the main concern of the Speleological Union of Ireland?

9. Who wrote of 'the dreary steeples of Fermanagh and Tyrone, emerging again'?

10. What is Talbot's Inch?

11. What is 'fionnadh bó'?

12. Who said this? "There won't be a cow milked in Clare tonight".

13. Glenveagh Castle and estate comprise Ireland's first example of?

14. What is the theme to *The Late Late Show*?

15. Who designed the videogame/ cartoon character *Earthworm Jim*?

Sport

answers on page 157

1. How many times in the 1970s did Ireland win rugby's Five Nations Championship?

2. Which rugby club does Keith Wood play for?

3. What was Irish rugby player Ian McLauchlan's nickname?

4. In which Olympics did Hugh Russell win a boxing Bronze medal for Ireland?

5. At which weight did Hugh Russell fight in the 1980 Olympics?

6. At which weight did Dave McAuley win Silver for Ireland?

7. In which Olympics did Dave McAuley did win a Silver medal?

8. In which boxing division did Michael Carruth win Olympic gold?

9. In which Olympics did Michael Carruth win a Gold medal?

10. In which Olympic event did Patrick O'Callaghan compete?

11. Which Newry man scored Aston Villa's winning goal in 1957's FA Cup final?

12. Which soccer manager altered Ireland's eligibilty rules?

13. Which Leeds United midfielder was part of Ireland's squad, April 2000?

14. In which sport is the McCarthy Cup contested?

15. When did Donegal win their first All-Ireland Senior football championship?

Natural History

answers on page 158

1. Which creatures would you find at Seaforde Gardens, Portaferry?

2. What date did Archbishop Ussher ascribe to Creation?

3. What contribution did Thomas Andrews FRS (1813-1885) make to world scientific knowledge?

4. Who built the 'Leviathan of Parsonstown'?

5. Creevykeel in Sligo has a megalithic court cairn. What does 'megalithic' mean?

6. Which Irish scientist might have been interested in the work of Prokofiev?

7. Peter Woulfe gave his name to an item of laboratory equipment. What was it?

8. When was Peter Woulfe born?

9. Which mathematical physicist was born in Magheragall, Antrim, 1857?

10. Which post connects Sir Joseph Larmor and Sir Isaac Newton?

11. If 'Skreen' were spelled 'Screen', in which county would George Stokes, physicist, have been born?

12. What was John Joly's main scientific interest?

13. Professor Thomas Romney Robinson invented which scientific instrument in 1843?

14. In which educational establishment was Robinson a professor?

15. Where was Francis Beaufort born?

Geography

answers on page 158

1. What is the shortest distance between Ireland and Scotland?

2. What was the capital of the ancient Province of Ulster?

3. In which Youghal house were the first potatoes planted in Ireland?

4. What is the county town of Laois?

5. What is the county town of Antrim?

6. Where was Lord Kitchener born?

7. Where would you find WB Yeats' Nobel Prize?

8. Where is Geneva?

9. Which mountain on the Dingle peninsula rises to 940 metres?

10. What height is reached by the Burren?

11. What is Bully's Acre?

12. Where is the 'marble city'?

13. What is the origin of the name 'Strangford' Lough?

14. Which county has an area of 896sq km?

15. Which county has an area of 2062sq km?

History

answers on page 158

1. How did James Connolly die?

2. When did Ireland enter the newly-formed United Kingdom?

3. What was the name of Erskine Childers' gun-running yacht?

4. Why was the secret society the 'Carders' so-called?

5. What took place 12th January 1603 at the mouth of the Liffey?

6. What movement began in 1791?

7. Where did Colonel Blood die?

8. In 1170, who was King of Connaught and High King of Ireland?

9. What were *inter Anglos* and *inter Hibernicos*?

10. For what in Dublin were Thomas Burke, Edward Lovett Pearce and James Gandon responsible?

11. When was Ireland last officially termed 'The Free State'?

12. Which of the rebels in 1916 had been a British colonial official and knight?

13. In which Irish shipyard was *Titanic* built?

14. Which ship of the Spanish Armada foundered off Dunluce Castle in 1588?

15. What was Lord Haw-Haw's hated 'catch-phrase'?

People

answers on page 158

1. Who financed a film of JM Synge's *Riders to the Sea*?

2. What was Constance Markiewicz's maiden name?

3. Which son of a former Lord Mayor of Dublin was involved heavily in World War II?

4. What was the full name of Lady Wilde?

5. Who said 'Work is the curse of the drinking classes'?

6. Whose words did he paraphrase?

7. Which Irish family's crest features 'an arm couped at the shoulder, embowed ppr., vested gu., holding in had a flag, sa., charged with a bee'?

8. What post did George Stoney hold?

9. When was John Dunlap (Dunlop) born?

10. What was Sean O'Casey's religion?

11. What was Ireland's population in 1911?

12. Which tragic figure is said to have given her name to Chapelizod, Dublin?

13. What does the suffix 'Óg' mean in a person's name?

14. Who was 'Humanity Dick'?

15. What does the Irish name 'Hickey' mean?

Specials

answers on page 159

1. What were the Hearts of Oak and the Hearts of Steel?

2. What was the 'Ulster Custom'?

3. What is Irish Spurge?

4. What is the difference between a 'bobby' and a 'peeler'?

5. What is the link between them?

6. What were Corry's Stars?

7. What opened in 1887 at Baltimore?

8. What name is shared by an 18th century writer and a former world squash champion?

9. What was the 'True Born Irishman' in 18th century Ireland?

10. Who was described as "the Spanish onion in the Irish stew"?

11. Which Irish hero met with Queen Victoria in 1871 after a third 'Waterloo' victory?

12. What was unusual about Master McGrath?

13. Which 'other' William and James, who share a surname if nothing else, are notorious, not for their battles, but for their words?

14. What is Pierce's Table?

15. What is 'Ireland's Saturday Night'?

Sport

answers on page 159

1. How many boxing medals did Ireland win in the 1984 Olympics?

2. Which Irishman won joint Bronze medal in boxing in the 1956 Olympics?

3. Who was John Caldwell's joint Bronze medallist in 1956?

4. What might qualify as Ireland's 'first' real Olympics?

5. What was notable about the Gaelic Football championships in 1999?

6. Which Everton defender was part of Ireland's squad, April 2000?

7. Which Fulham player was part of Ireland's squad, April 2000?

8. Which Irish golf course was designed by Christy O'Connor Jr.?

9. When was the Irish Football Association formed?

10. Where was the Irish Football Association formed?

11. What was Ireland's first football club?

12. In what year were Bohemians founded in Dublin?

13. What sport is played by Bohemians?

14. Which sport was ruled by the Irish Football Union, in November 1874?

15. What unusual article did DB Walkington wear while playing for Ireland in 1887?

Television

answers on page 159

1. Eamonn Andrews presented which television show dedicated to the achievements of celebrities?

2 What is the short name of the Irish language TV station?

3. What was the first RTÉ 'soap opera'?

4. What is the name of RTÉ 'agricultural soap'?

5. When did regular TV broadcasting begin in Ireland?

6. Which one-time Director of Britain's Channel Four became President of Ireland?

7. For which television company did Mary McAleese once work as a journalist and presenter?

8. What happens on RTÉ 1 television at 6pm, for 1 minute?

9. James Ellis starred in which 1960s British police drama?

10. Which character did Colm Meaney play in several *Star Trek* series'?

11. Who played *Father Ted*'s housekeeper, Mrs.Doyle?

12. What is the family connection between *Ballykissangel* and *Drop the Dead Donkey*?

13. Which actor links *Ballykissangel* and *Drop the Dead Donkey*?

14. Which television series did future Bond Pierce Brosnan star in?

15. Where is the soap opera *Fair City* set?

Industry

answers on page 160

1. What is significant about W. Collins and Co.?

2. Who founded Guinness' Brewery in 1759?

3. When did the transatlantic telegraph cable cease operation to Valentia Island?

4. What was unusual about *Olympic*?

5. Name the paddle steamers which crossed the Irish Sea in 1860?

6. In 1885 the four paddle steamers were joined by another. Its name?

7. What was licensed in Tramore Bay in 1862?

8. Which aptly named gentleman gained a license for oyster beds in Cork harbour, 1860s?

9. As well as being eaten, what was seaweed once used as?

10. What was the name of the U-boat sunk by *Olympic*?

11. When did Ferguson Tractor Company merge with Massey to become Massey-Ferguson?

12. What links the Dublin buildings, Boland's Mill and Jacob's Biscuit Factory historically?

13. Which internet search engine owes its name to the imagination of Dean Swift?

14. For which fabric is Donegal most famous for?

15. Which industrialist made the Glenveagh Castle estate the marvel it is today?

Geography

answers on page 160

1. Where was Victor McLaglen born?

2. What was the capital of the ancient kingdom of Ossory?

3. What is the derivation of the placename Brittas?

4. What is the highest point in Ulster?

5. Where was St. Columba baptised?

6. What is the county town of Limerick?

7. What is the county town of Clare?

8. Leitrim, Roscommon and Mayo share a border with which county?

9. Where was Maureen O'Sullivan, actress, born?

10. Through which county does the river Derry flow?

11. Where was future President Erskine Childers born?

12. Why is 'Joyce's Country' in Co. Galway so-called?

13. Where is Kilmogue Dolmen?

14. In which city was de Valera born?

15. In which county is Birr Castle?

History

answers on page 160

1. Which seat of government did Robert Emmet attack?

2. How many famines did nineteenth century Ireland experience before the Great Famine?

3. In 1880, who was the High Sherriff of Wicklow?

4. What was built on Belfast's Falls Road in 1829?

5. Which ancient kingdom spanned Ireland and Scotland?

6. In what year was Trinity College, Dublin, founded?

7. Why was Cobh renamed Queenstown?

8. How many ships were in the French fleet with Wolfe Tone in 1796?

9. How many of these ships landed in Ireland?

10. Which country did Haakon IV rule?

11. What did the 1366 Statutes of Kilkenny generally prohibit?

12. Who was the first Earl of Ranelagh?

13. When was Ireland first termed 'The Free State'?

14. A memorial to the Irish dead of which war was placed in Dublin's Methodist Centenary Church?

15. What was the original name of the area which is now Phoenix Park?

Music

answers on page 160

1. In which group does Roisin Murphy sing?

2. When was the Ash album '1977' released?

3. Which 2 television series with Christian names in title featured Clannad's music?

4. Who has been called 'Ireland's Queen of Country'?

5. Which Irish singer co-manages Westlife?

6. In which year did Dana win the Eurovision Song Contest?

7. How many times has Ireland won the Eurovision Song Contest?

8. Who sang *Rock and Roll Kids*, Ireland's winner in Eurovision Song Contest in 1994?

9. When was the *Soldier's Song* written?

10. Which Irish song is also a James Joyce novel?

11. The name of the band 'Moloko' comes from which Anthony Burgess novel?

12. Which Irish group took its name from a famous United Irishman?

13. Which instrument does Derek Bell play?

14. Where do the Clancy Brothers come from?

15. Complete the line 'Low lie the fields of...'?

People

answers on page 161

1. What does JM stand for in JM Synge?

2. Which Irish actor appeared in a double act with a horse in the film *The Quiet Man*?

3. Who founded the Peace People?

4. Which international honour were the two founders of the Peace People awarded?

5. Who founded St. Enda's School, Dublin?

6. Rowel Friers is famous as?

7. Who killed Strongbow?

8. In which language was Eileen O'Leary's *The Lament for Art O'Leary* written?

9. Who owned the Co. Mayo estates managed by the infamous Charles Cunningham Boycott?

10. Who was 'Ephemera'?

11. Who was first accepted into Trinity College Dublin from 1793?

12. As what is Father Theobald Mathew remembered?

13. What did he establish?

14. Who first prepared 'Irish coffee'?

15. By whose reckoning was a journey from Galway - St.John's, Newfoundland "the shortest route between this country and America"?

Specials

answers on page 161

1. What was a 'croppy'?

2. Why was Dun Laoghaire re-named 'Kingstown'?

3. Tambour and run are types of which decorative work?

4. What does the Latin phrase 'hiberniores hibernis ipsos' mean?

5. Which word can be both an accent and a shoe?

6. On which English college was Trinity College Dublin based?

7. What happened to the 'Empress of Ireland' in 1914?

8. What was set up in Oughterard in 1852?

9. What was 'kelp' used for?

10. Why was 'kelp' necessary for these processes?

11. What were the 'Blueshirts'?

12. What was the 'Sixth of George I'?

13. What was 'Cumann na nGaedhael'?

14. What was 'an tSlighe Mhór'?

15. What was the Severe Pine Tree Buttress?

Sport

answers on page 161

1. How many players-a-side contested the 1887 All-Ireland Hurling final?

2. How many medals did Ireland win in 1928, its first Olympics as a Republic?

3. How many medals did Ireland win in the 1956 Olympics?

4. How many medals did Ireland win in the 1980 Olympics?

5. When did John Treacy win silver in the Olympic Marathon?

6. What was John Treacy's time for the Marathon at the 1984 Olympics?

7. Which Irishman retained his sport's Olympic title, one of three men to do so?

8. Which Irishman won joint Bronze medal in boxing in 1980 Olympics?

9. Who was joint Bronze medallist with boxer Hugh Russell in 1980?

10. Which medal did boxer Wayne McCullough win in 1992?

11. Who beat Wayne McCullough to win Olympic Gold in 1992?

12. At which boxing weight did Wayne McCullough compete?

13. Ireland's soccer team sometimes features players not born in Ireland. Why?

14. George Best is famous as a player for which football club?

15. Which world-famous rugby side did Munster beat in 1978?

Theatre

answers on page 162

1. Which playwright is famous for *Philadelphia Here I Come?*

2. Who wrote the play *The Playboy of the Western World?*

3. Where was actor Liam Neeson born?

4. Which Séan O'Casey character is the Captain's sidekick?

5. Which O'Casey play takes its title from a worker's flag?

6. Name of the main female character in Sean O'Casey's play *Juno and the Paycock?*

7. Which Irish dramatist was awarded the Nobel Prize in 1925?

8. What was the original title of Dublin's Abbey Theatre?

9. What is a 'paycock', as in *Juno and the Paycock?*

10. Where was Samuel Beckett's *Waiting for Godot* first performed?

11. Where was actor Cyril Cusack born?

12. Who founded Dublin's Abbey Theatre?

13. Which American situation comedy shares its title with a Samuel Beckett play?

14. Who wrote *Krapp's Last Tape?*

15. Which Irish playwright wrote *The Field?*

Geography

answers on page 162

1. What is the picturesque title of the subterranean limestone caves found near Florencecourt, Co. Fermanagh?

2. One of the earliest human habitations in Ireland were termed Early and Late Larnian, after which Irish town?

3. What is the county town of Kerry?

4. What is the county town of Kilkenny?

5. What is the county town of Dublin?

6. Where was Ernest Shackleton born?

7. Where was Ernest Shackleton buried?

8. Where is the Nore Valley?

9. Where is WB Yeats buried?

10. In which county is Cape Clear?

11. What is the largest fresh water expanse in the British Isles?

12. Where was Thomas McDonough, executed in 1916, born?

13. In which county is Muckish Mountain?

14. Which province lends its name to a cloth overcoat?

15. Where was 'Devil' Dill born?

History

answers on page 162

1. What do the initials IRB stand for?

2. What do the initials IRA stand for?

3. What do the initials ICA stand for?

4. On which common date were the IRB and Fenian Brotherhood founded?

5. Which country did a group calling itself the 'Irish Republican Army' enter unlawfully in summer 1866?

6. What did RIC stand for?

7. What did the RIC become in the 1920s?

8. What was the Irish police called?

9. Which building opened 1st August, 1906?

10. What did GNR stand for in 19th century Ireland?

11. When was Trinity College, Dublin founded?

12. When was University College Dublin founded?

13. Who introduced coinage into Ireland?

14. When was Queenstown renamed?

15. What was the name of the British ship captured by John Barry?

People

answers on page 162

1. On whose life was the film *The General* based?

2. What in Ireland is 'The Holy Land'?

3. Who said 'If I knew who Godot was, I would have said so'?

4. When was Ireland's first 'test-tube baby' born?

5. When was the third Nobel Peace Prize awarded to Irish people?

6. In which field was William Dargan (1799-1867), famous?

7. Who founded the Stud Farm which became the National Stud?

8. Who were the 'Four Masters'?

9. Which Irishman was a pioneer of the agricultural tractor?

10. Who was curate at Boolavogue in April 1798, during the Rising?

11. Who was the First Earl of Athlone?

12. Which Irish philosopher had a Californian city named after him in 1866, 113 years after his death?

13. Who was the first Earl of Portarlington?

14. Which English designer and architect planned the gardens at Heywood?

15. Which famous designer was involved in the preparation of the gardens at Heywood?

Religion

answers on page 163

1. Which cleric ordained singer Sinead O'Connor a priest?

2. From which precious metal was the Ardagh Chalice fashioned?

3. Which 'relic' of St. Oliver Plunkett, an Irish bishop executed in England, survives?

4. Where is this relic to be found?

5. Who was the first papal legate to Ireland?

6. Pope Adrian VI granted Ireland to which English king in 1155?

7. What was Henry Joy McCracken's religion?

8. Who buried St. Patrick?

9. What is St Brigid's feast day?

10. Against whom would Irish monks recite 'A furore Normanorum libera nos, Domine'?

11. The pilgrimage site at Knock has an amenity denied many less famous sites. What is it?

12. Which military group met Pope Pius XII on 12th June 1944?

13. When was Mellifont Abbey founded?

14. Which monastic order founded Kilcooly Abbey in Tipperary?

15. What was the year of 'Catholic Emancipation'?

Specials

answers on page 163

1. What became illegal in Ireland on 28 February 1935?

2. On which date did Dublin catch up with London?

3. Arklow in Co. Wicklow was the first place in Ireland to have which life-saving service?

4. Which organisation participated in a demonstration sport in the 4th modern Olympics?

5. What can be found at 53° 00' N, 8° 00' W?

6. What are the Gobbins?

7. Which type of race takes place near Cape Clear?

8. What are the North and South Slobs?

9. "'I do not know', said the man, 'what the custom of the English may be, but it is the custom of the Irish to hate villains.'" From which nineteenth century novel is this quote taken?

10. What is a 'turlough'?

11. Where was the first 'Irish coffee' produced?

12. What is a coracle?

13. Who were the 'Molly Maguires'?

14. What does RDS stand for?

15. What is boxty?

Sport

answers on page 163

1. When was the Irish Ladies' Hockey Union founded?

2. Which international rally event did Paddy Hopkirk write a book about?

3. The Irish Football Union and which other formed the Irish Rugby Football Union?

4. When was this union formed?

5. Why would DB Walkington, rugby player, never be far from a quiz?

6. Ireland beat a world-class side on 2nd July 1969. In which sport?

7. Which team did Ireland defeat?

8. In which Irish town did this match take place?

9. Which sport first took hold in Ireland in Cork during 1880s?

10. When was the first fully documented match of women's cricket in Ireland?

11. Dalkey Quarry was an important development site in which sport?

12. Between which teams was the first Hockey international played?

13. Who won this match?

14. Where was the match played?

15. Phil Casey of Mountrath was the first world champion in which sport, in 1889?

Theatre

answers on page 164

1. The great actress Siobhan McKenna is best known for which role in JM Synge's *Playboy of the Western World*?

2. What is the name of the main male character in Sean O'Casey's *Juno and the Paycock*?

3. Which Irish President has had a play staged in Dublin's Gaiety Theatre?

4. Who starred with Michael Flatley in the original *Riverdance*?

5. Which play caused riots in Dublin, 1907?

6. Who wrote a play based on the tragedy of Ellen Hanley?

7. Who wrote the comic play *The Whiteheaded Boy*?

8. Who wrote the play *The Shadow of a Gunman*?

9. Christy Mahon is the title character in which JM Synge play?

10. Where was Brian Friel born?

11. Which playwright has one of his characters cry 'Take away our hearts of stone and give us hearts of flesh'?

12. Which city features in one of Brian Friel's most famous plays?

13. Who said "thank you sister, may you be mother to a bishop"?

14. What age was Krapp when he made his 'last tape'?

15. Who wrote the play, *The Informer*?

Politics

answers on page 164

1. When did Garret Fitzgerald become Taoiseach?

2. How many consecutive terms may an Irish president serve?

3. Which Sinn Fein member was minister for Education in Northern Ireland Assembly?

4. How many Westminster MPs are elected from Northern Ireland?

5. When was the IRA declared illegal in Ireland?

6. Who was to represent Co. Down in the first Dail?

7. When was Sinn Féin formed?

8. When was Cumann na nGaedhael formed?

9. When did Cumann na nGaedhael cease to exist. Why?

10. Which post did John Costello hold at this time?

11. Who was the first leader of the DUP?

12. What is the literal translation of 'Sinn Fein'?

13. What does DUP stand for?

14. Which modern political party developed from Cumann na nGaedheal?

15. Who founded the Fenian Brotherhood in US?

Arts

answers on page 164

1. Which weekly newspaper did Thomas Osborne Davis help found?

2. Who became the editor after his death?

3. Which poet and artist described himself as 'an Irishman of planter stock, by profession an art gallery man'?

4. Which artist was a leading producer Irish stained glass work?

5. Where did Thomas Davis writeabout the importance of 'National poetry'?

6. Which Irish ballet dancer founded the ballet company which became the Royal Ballet?

7. John Joly also pioneered which art form?

8. Where was Dame Ninette De Valois born?

9. What was Dame Ninette De Valois originally named?

10. What was the name of the first American daily newspaper?

11. In what area of life was Nathaniel Hone notable?

12. Edwin Hayes painted a picture showing Ireland's loss. Its title?

13. Which Dublin-born artist created a 15,000 sq. feet work of art in an Edinburgh church late in the 19th century?

14. In which artistic field was John Hickey famous?

15. In which artistic field was Thomas Hickey famous?

Films

answers on page 164

1. Liam Neeson was Oscar-nominated for which film?

2. Which 1999 film by Alan Parker starred two Scottish actors as Irish parents?

3. Which film by the production team behind *Trainspotting* and *Shallow Grave* had a hit song from the northern Irish band Ash?

4. In which film does Colm Meaney play a harassed Dublin father?

5. Which film featured a horse called Tir na nÓg?

6. Bob Geldof starred as a rock musician in which Alan Parker film?

7. *Still Crazy*, a film about a British rock group's comeback, starred which Irish actor?

8. What is the name of Victor McLaglen's character in *The Quiet Man*?

9. What is Maureen O'Hara's character called in *The Quiet Man*?

10. How did Sean Thornton make a living before returning to Ireland?

11. Richard Harris starred in which famous rugby film?

12. For which Irish film did Brenda Fricker win an Academy Award?

13. What nationality are the male and female leads in Alan Parker's *Angela's Ashes*?

14. Which 'Prime Suspect' did John Lynch star alongside in *Cal*?

15. Which Irish folk hero did Liam Neeson play in a Neil Jordan film?

Geography

answers on page 165

1. Which town in Derry is the birthplace of the man who announced the American Declaration of Independence?

2. What is the county town of Cork?

3. What is the county town of Westmeath?

4. Tyrone, Fermanagh and Leitrim share a border with which county?

5. Magilligan Point and Greencastle are found to the north of which body of water?

6. Where was Patrick Kavanagh born?

7. Between which towns did Charles Bianconi's stage network first run?

8. Where is Crookhaven?

9. Which Kildare town is also a part of the leg?

10. Which river flows into Dublin Bay at Clontarf?

11. Which county has an area of 2338sq km?

12. Which county has an area of 3188sq km?

13. Which county has an area of 2025sq km?

14. What separates Ireland from Wales?

15. In which county is Ardagh, famous for the golden chalice?

History

answers on page 165

1. What did the Times call O'Connell's mass gatherings?

2. From what were women exempted by the Synod of Tara, 697 AD?

3. Scarva in Co. Down holds what on 13th July each year?

4. Where was the Irish terminal of the Atlantic cable?

5. Why was the Atlantic cable laid successfully in 1866?

6. Of which town was Sir Walter Raleigh warden from 1588-89?

7. When was Crumlin Road Gaol completed?

8. When was the University of Cork founded?

9. Who said in 1896 "I am resolved to take whatever course is best for Ireland"?

10. Who said that 'The repeal of the External Relations Act will take the gun out of Irish politics'?

11. Which event was Jim Larkin most famous for participating in?

12. Who were attacked in Limerick in 1904?

13. What was the former name of Dublin's O'Connell Street?

14. Which British naval hero once had a monument on Dublin's O'Connell Street?

15. When did the first flight take place from Dublin Airport?

People

answers on page 165

1. Liam Neeson is married to which English actress?

2. Which Irish naval explorer was the first to travel the North West Passage?

3. Which famous Irishman was nephew to Eileen O'Leary?

4. What was Frank O'Connor's real name?

5. Who was offered the rule of Ireland in 1263?

6. Who was the first woman to steam across the Atlantic?

7. Who described Sir William Ferguson as "some ancient sea-king sitting among the inland wheat and poppies"?

8. Who was known as the 'Long Fellow'?

9. Who wrote "Ireland, as distinct from her people, is nothing to me"?

10. Who was Molly Maguire?

11. What does 'Colmcille' mean?

13. Who was known as St Richard of Dundalk?

14. What is the Irish meaning of the name 'Aherne' or 'Ahern'?

15. The 'Aherne' family crest shows three animals - what are they?

Specials

answers on page 166

1. How many men play on a hurling side?

2. What were the 'Wild Geese'?

3. What is a 'shillelagh' commonly thought to be?

4. Where does this term come from?

5. In 1956 there were at least 2 packs of staghounds operating in Ireland. Name two.

6. Which distinction did Ireland share with Belarus before the 2000 Olympics?

7. What was a 'Teltown marriage'?

8. What spends 6 months of every year on Wexford Harbour's North Slob?

9. When was the collared dove introduced to Ireland?

10. What are Kilkenny Cats?

11. What do the 'Walls of Limerick' and 'The Bridge of Athlone' have in common?

12. Where did the word 'navvie' originate?

13. Which literary, radio, comic strip and film character has been played by an Englishman, Scotsman, Australian, and most recently by an Irishman?

14. What is 'The Point'?

15. What is fadge?

Sport

answers on page 166

1. What was the GAA invasion of USA in 1886?

2. What distance did Ireland's first Gordon-Bennett race cover?

3. When was Ireland's first Gordon-Bennett race cover?

4. Which event was the subject of sports' first radio commentary?

5. When was the first Irish rugby international?

6. Where was this match held?

7. When did Ireland first win rugby's 'Triple Crown'?

8. The 1896 rugby side touring South Africa gave rise to which coincidence?

9. Which Irish rugby player was imprisoned over the disappearance of an Argentinian flag in 1980?

10. What did Ireland win in 1932, for the first time in 33 years?

11. Which Irish rugby international also had Olympic importance?

12. Which rugby player said "I hate small men"?

13. When did Willie John McBride score his first international try?

14. When was the McCarthy Cup first presented in gaelic games?

15. After whom is the Cup named?

Natural History

answers on page 166

1. Which animal is called broc in Irish?

2. What is *neotinea intacta*?

3. Which Irish dog is characterised by thick brown curly fur and a 'rat-like' tail?

4. Which Irish Dog was bred to hunt deer?

5. Which Irish dog was bred to hunt wolves?

6. Which Irish dog is named for a county and a colour?

7. Which Irish newspaper shares its name with an Irish dish?

8. Which son of the Ist Earl of Cork is important to chemistry?

9. What is Boyle's Law?

10. What was the name of the 19th century telescope at Birr Castle?

11. In which university is the Guy Heywood Daffodil Garden?

12. To which Irishman do we owe the book *The Origin of Species*?

13. Against which skin complaint was Irish Spurge sometimes used?

14. Which measurement of windspeed is named after an Irishman?

15. Which bird gives its name to Mullary Cross in Co. Louth?

Literature

answers on page 166

1. Where was Frank McCourt born?

2. Which Irish writer is best known as a Canadian citizen?

3. Which honour was author William Trevor awarded in 1977?

4. With what was Thomas Prior's 'List of the Absentees of Ireland' concerned?

5. Which James Joyce novel follows the life of Stephen Dedalus?

6. Who wrote the novel *The Collegians*?

7. Who wrote the novel *Strumpet City*?

8. According to Brendan Behan, what is "an author's first duty"?

9. Which footballer's autobiography was entitled *Attack*?

10. What, according to the title of his book, did Chevalier Jacques De Latocnaye do in 1796-7?

11. What has been modified in Joyce's use of the song title 'Finnegan's Wake', for his novel?

12. When was Lawrence Sterne born?

13. For which book is Lawrence Sterne most famous?

14. What was the title of Christopher Nolan's autobiography?

15. What is the name of the Finnegan in *Finnegans Wake*?

Films

answers on page 167

1. Which soccer superstar is profiled in the film *Best*?

2. For which Steven Soderburgh film did David Holmes provide the soundtrack?

3. Which computer animated film used the Thin Lizzy song *The Boys are Back in Town*?

4. Which film starring Samuel L. Jackson and Geena Davis features an Irish water spaniel?

5. Complete the title of a Peter O'Toole film - *My Favourite...*?

6. How many times has Peter O'Toole been nominated for an Academy Award?

7. How many Academy Awards has Peter O'Toole received?

8. Which film by the Coen brothers starred Gabriel Byrne?

9. Tom Berenger co-starred with which Irish actor in *The Field*?

10. Who directed the film *Best*?

11. Mary McGuckian is married to which Irish actor?

12. What was the title of the film which Liam Neeson played Michael Collins?

13. Which Irish-born actor links the Antichrist and dinosaurs?

14. Which Irish actress starred in both *Hear My Song* and *Sirens*?

15. What is Hollywood's most famous 'donnybrook'?

Geography

answers on page 167

1. What was the capital of the ancient Province of Connacht?

2. Where was Lady Wilde, mother to the writer, born?

3. What is the county town of Galway?

4. What is the county town of Meath?

5. From which county did Lory Meagher hail?

6. In which county are the Curlew Mountains?

7. Which is the O'Moore County?

8. What is the meaning of the 'border town', Muff, in Donegal?

9. What is Donegal's Knockalla Mountain is also known as?

10. On which hill did Ireland's fair maids vie for the honour of being Finn MacCool's wife?

11. How large an area do the Burren Hills of Clare cover?

12. Which county has an area of 4380sq km?

13. Where is Boolavogue?

14. Which Irish county was divided into North and South Ridings?

15. In which city was JB Dunlop born?

History

answers on page 167

1. When was Dublin's O'Connell Bridge built?

2. What was O'Connell Bridge originally called?

3. When was O'Connell Bridge renamed?

4. When did Ernest Shackleton first visit the Antarctic?

5. How near the South Pole did Shackleton get in 1907?

6. When did Molly Malone die?

7. What is the term attached to 30th January 1972?

8. When was building of the Royal Belfast Academical Institution completed?

9. Which event coincided with the passing of Ireland's External Relations Act, 11th December 1936?

10. Who wrote of the Dublin Lockout, 11th September 1913: "People are thrown into prison for making the most peaceful speeches. The city is like an armed camp"?

11. When and where was William Joyce born?

12. Which Irishman broadcast Nazi propaganda during World War II?

13. William Joyce was more commonly known as?

14. What was unusual about Lord Haw-Haw's fate?

15. Who commanded the Jacobite and Williamite forces at Aughrim?

People

answers on page 168

1. Which important equestrian figure once lived in Grangemellon Castle near Levitstown Crossroads, Co. Kildare?

2. Who founded the RIC in 1814?

3. When did JM Synge die?

4. Who developed Mullaghmore Harbour in the nineteenth century?

5. Who wrote of Countess Markiewicz that she was 'a haggard woman returned'?

6. What did Joseph Plunkett's father do in 1917, recalling the actions of Constance Markiewicz?

7. John Z. De Lorean. What did the Z. stand for?

8. Traditionally, when is the last day of the Irish summer?

9. What was the French motto of O'Brien, Earl of Thomond?

10. What does this motto mean in English?

11. Which of the founders of the *Titanic*'s shipyard lived to see the ship?

12. What are the full names of Harland and Wolff?

13. When did Edward Harland die?

14. When did Gustave Wolff die?

15. Which non-royal Irish family included a 'Prince' among them?

Specials

answers on page 168

1. Who once wrote that 'The Famine knocked the heart out of the Irish language'?

2. What is notable about the South Pole Inn in Annascaul, Co. Kerry?

3. Which college educated both Jonathan Swift and Oliver Goldsmith?

4. Little Skellig island has Ireland's largest concentration of which animal?

5. What is Great Saltee?

6. What would an Irish Tory have been accused of?

7. What is a Tory today?

8. What were the Four Masters responsible for?

9. What is the international dialling code for Dublin?

10. What was a pitch-cap?

11. What was entitled 'LIBERTY, EQUALITY, FRATERNITY, UNION!'?

12. When was Dun Laoghaire re-named 'Kingstown'?

13. At 270m long and 28m high, what in 1912 was the world's largest man-made mobile object?

14. What is Lisdoonvarna famous for?

15. What does USPCA stand for?

Sport

answers on page 168

1. Which team have Jennings, O'Leary and Stapleton played for?

2. Which Irish soccer internationals of the same name ended their careers 41 years apart?

3. Who was the first Irish woman to take part in an Olympic swimming final?

4. What sort of race was Gordon-Bennett?

5. When did Roscommon win their first All Ireland Senior Final?

6. When did the first Northern Ireland team win the Sam Maguire Cup?

7. Which team won the Sam Maguire Cup in 1960?

8. How many consecutive softball titles did Michael (Duxie) Walsh win up to 1993?

9. Which sports did Wembley Stadium first host in May 1958?

10. Which teams played in these matches?

11. Which 2 footballers played for 2 teams on the same day in 1957?

12. Which teams did these footballers play for?

13. Who wrote "My Road to Victory", published in 1987?

14. Which sport used to include scores of 'Horsemen', 'Tally' and 'Look sharp'?

15. Which sport was United Irishman Michael Boylan, of Blakestown, Ardee, playing when he was arrested?

Geography

answers on page 168

1. What is the main function of Silent Valley in Co. Down?

2. What is the county town of Kildare?

3. What is the county town of Donegal?

4. What is Northern Ireland's smallest county?

5. What are Gowlaun, Twins and Rathbaum?

6. What is Feohanagh, Limerick's 'Scottish' connection?

7. Where are the Twelve Bens?

8. What is the origin of Draperstown?

9. Which county has an area of 2108sq km?

10. Which county has an area of 1551sq km?

11. Where was the First Earl of Athlone born?

12. What number of Aran Islands are there?

13. When did rail travel begin from Belfast to Dublin?

14. Where in Donegal did the kings of Ulster once hold court?

15. Where is the Yellow Ford?

History

answers on page 169

1. On what date did the IRA announce in Dublin that it had ended the terrorist campaign which it had carried out against Northern Ireland since December 1956?

2. What was the name given to the Celtic 'senate'?

3. When was the first full Irish Constitution enacted?

4. Eamon de Valera was President of the council of which forerunner to the United Nations, in September 1932?

5. On what date did Eire withdraw from the British Commonwealth?

6. When was the first Northern Ireland parliament opened?

7. Éamon de Valera offered condolence at the death of which leader?

8. When did Liam T. Cosgrave die?

9. When did President John F. Kennedy visit Ireland?

10. Which council did Ireland join on 1st January 1960?

11. When was Éamon de Valera elected President of Ireland?

12. When did Ireland join the United Nations?

13. On what date was the Garda Siochana established in law?

14. When was the 'Irish Free State' admitted to the League of Nations?

15. When were the first Free State postage stamps issued?

People

answers on page 169

1. After whom was Croke Park named?

2. Who founded the Royal Canadian Mounted Police?

3. Who travelled under the pseudonym 'Sebastian Melmoth'?

4. What was Ireland's population in 1991?

5. Who was 'Wolfe Tone MacGowan'?

6. What was Eamon De Valera's given name?

7. To which group of languages does Irish belong?

8. What is Ireland's national airline?

9. Which heraldic crest is described 'issuing out of a cloud, a dexter arm, embowed brandishing a sword all propr.'?

10. What was the motto of O'Brien, Earl of Thomond?

11. What does this motto mean in English?

12. What is the Irish motto of Baron O'Neill, of Shane's Castle, Antrim?

13. What is this motto's English translation?

14. What was the profession of Edward Carson's father?

15. Who said "English is the native language of Irishmen"?

Specials

answers on page 169

1. Where was the starting point of the first east-to-west solo Atlantic flight?

2. Which county Carlow house brings to mind a notorious American music festival?

3. What is the female equivalent of the sport of hurling?

4. What was *cervus megaseros*?

5. Who or what is known as the "Queen of the Nine Glens"?

6. Who was Danu?

7. Where did 'boycott' originate?

8. What is 'champ'?

9. Kimberly and Mikado are famous as what?

10. Who are the 'Saffrons'?

11. Which county might be seen as somewhat depressed?

12. What is the dialling code for Northern Ireland?

13. What were 'the races of Castlebar'?

14. Why was it called 'the races of Castlebar'?

15. Where was Shergar stabled when he was kidnapped?

Geography

answers on page 170

1. How were 6 new counties created in 1608?

2. Where would you find Two Rock Mountain and Three Rock Mountain?

3. What is the county town of Offaly?

4. Kerry, Limerick, Tipperary and Waterford share a border with which county?

5. Which county in Leinster is the only one without a coastline?

6. Where is Fastnet Rock?

7. Where is Bonamargy Abbey?

8. Which county has an area of 1326sq km?

9. Which county has an area of 5939sq km?

10. Which county has an area of 2000sq km?

11. Where was Thomas D'Arcy McGee born?

12. What is the motto of Mullaghgane, Antrim?

13. Where is Armagh Observatory situated?

14. Where was Trinity College, Dublin founded?

15. Where was John Barry born?

Sport

answers on page 170

1. When was Ireland's first Olympic Games?

2. Where is the Irish 2,000 Guineas run?

3. What do John Watson's first and last season's have in common?

4. Which sport was played by JJ Bowles?

5. The Irish rugby team of 1887 fielded the son of which gothic novelist?

6. What age was the racehorse Shergar when he was kidnapped?

7. Which English classic race did Shergar win twice?

8. Which Irish soccer star missed the London premiere of the film *Best*?

9. Which Irish emigrant won Gold for USA in 1920 Olympics?

10. In which event did Patrick J. Ryan win Olympic gold?

11. What sport did Tony O'Reilly, business magnate play for Ireland?

12. How many caps did Tony O'Reilly win?

13. How many caps did David O'Leary win with Ireland's football team?

14. Who was the first man to win seven All-Ireland medals?

15. Who became world flyweight boxing champion in 1947?

Geography

answers on page 170

1. Where was the publisher of America's first daily newspaper born?

2. What is the county town of Wicklow?

3. Where did Ireland's last-known prosecuted witch come from?

4. What is the better-known name of Tandragee Castle?

5. Which county has an area of 1851sq km?

6. Which county has an area of 1890sq km?

7. Which county has an area of 1838sq km?

8. What does Cavan mean in Irish?

9. What can be found at Lissyviggeen?

10. In which county did the kings of Ulster once hold court?

11. Which ports were served by the 'province' steamers?

12. What is the current name of this street?

13. What is the highest point in Co. Wicklow?

14. How long is the Carrick-a-rede rope bridge?

15. In which county was Rory Gallagher born?

Specials

answers on page 170

1. What was the *Sirius*, and what is its connection to Cork?

2. What is 'dulse'?

3. Which animal was once featured on the reverse of an Irish ten pence coin?

4. What are 'The Waves of Tory'?

5. What was the land speed record set in Ireland, July 1903?

6. What were the 'Drapier's Letters'?

7. Who wrote the 'Drapier's Letters'?

8. Who is Phildy Hackball?

9. Who traditionally hunted the small birds?

10. What do *Anacreon* and *Hoche* have in common?

11. What did the phrase 'hard word' mean in 19th century Ireland?

12. What special type of bridge spanned Dublin's Royal Canal?

13. A Wild Duck, not a Wild Goose made John Barry a famous sailor. Why?

14. What award did Cedric Gibbons receive 'for consistent excellence'?

15. What is Fairyhouse?

Sport

answers on page 171

1. When did Ireland first compete in the Winter Olympics?

2. Who won the World Cup of golf with Paul McGinley in 1997?

3. On which island did Paul McGinley and Padraig Harrington win golf World Cup 1997?

4. Which Irish President was once a substitute Irish rugby fullback?

5. Who was the first Ulsterman to head the GAA?

6. Why was 1890's Munster Senior Football final abandoned after 57 minutes?

7. Between which teams was the 1890 Munster Senior Football final contested?

8. Why was the 1899 Cork vs Tipperary match abandoned at half-time?

9. What is unusual about 1900 and 1902 Connacht Senior finals?

10. When was Derry's first All-Ireland Senior Football title?

11. Who was Derry's captain in 1993 Senior Final?

12. Who was the youngest ever player in an FA Cup Final?

13. In which sport did Lory Meagher become famous?

14. For which county side did Lory Meagher play hurling?

15. Who became IBF world flyweight champion in 1989?

Geography

answers on page 171

1. Which river valleys converge at the Meeting of the Waters?

2. What is the county town of Armagh?

3. Which county in Connacht is the only one without a coastline?

4. Ireland is roughly the size of which American state?

5. Which Kerry area was once described as 'Heaven's reflex'?

6. What is the importance of Great Saltee, Clare Island and Lambay Island?

7. Near which Armagh church is Brian Boru supposedly buried?

8. What is the name of the English nuclear power station closest to Ireland?

9. Which county has an area of 1795sq km?

10. Which county has an area of 4701sq km?

11. Where was Michael Collins imprisoned after the Rising?

12. How high was the dome of Dublin's Custom House?

13. What sort of ancient monument can be found near Clogher, Co. Tyrone?

14. Where is Lough Furnace?

15. St. Patrick's Church of Ireland stands on two branches of which Dublin river?

Specials

answers on page 171

1. Which Irish county shares its name with a buoyant wood?

2. What principally connects Killyleagh Co. Down with the British Museum?

3. Why is Rathlin an Irish island, rather than Scottish?

4. What is the origin of Donegal's The Frosses?

5. What is Dublin's North Bull?

6. What are the Paps of Danu?

7. What are pampooties?

8. Which world record was set between Athy, Co. Kildare and Phoenix Park, July 1903?

9. What is the main alcohol ingredient in Irish coffee?

10. What ransom was demanded for the return of Shergar?

11. Of which country is Daniel O'Donnell an 'honorary citizen'?

12. What is 'keening'?

13. Who would have sung 'Croppies Lie Down'?

14. Who or what was Spring Rice?

15. What is the Tour of the Sperrins?

Sport

answers on page 172

1. When did Stephen Roche win the Tour de France?

2. Which sport do Shelbourne play?

3. Players and staff of which sport are eligible for the Tom Rooney Award?

4. Dave Gallaher was the first captain of which world-beating rugby side?

5. Where did Dave Gallaher come from?

6. In which sport did Youghal's Cally Riordan play in junior and senior All Ireland finals?

7. What was unusual about these competitions?

8. Who played camogie for Dublin across 3 decades?`

9. Paul Russell, a Kerryman, represented which province in 1927?

10. Which province did Paul Russell represent in 1928?

11. What age was Norman Whiteside when he played in his first FA Cup Final?

12. What was unusual about Ireland manager Jack Charlton?

13. Which Northern Ireland manager had a stadium named after him?

14. Who was the first Irishman to reach the summit of Mount Everest?

15. Which year saw Dennis Taylor become snooker World Champion?

Geography

answers on page 172

1. From which mountain is the Rock of Cashel said to have come?

2. Meath, Dublin, Wicklow, Carlow, Laois, Offaly and Westmeath share a border with which county?

3. Where is the town of Mooncoin?

4. In which county is Stillorgan?

5. Which county has an area of 1719sq km?

6. Which city was described as being 'Built on reclaimed mud, hammers playing in the shipyard'?

7. Which counties comprised the Kingdom of Dal Riada?

8. What are the stones in the Lissyviggeen circle also known as?

9. Where was scientist John Tyndall born?

10. Name the final port of call of the liner *Titanic*?

11. Where did John Redmond die?

12. What was the name of the street in which Wolfe Tone was born?

13. Which county claims Daniel O'Donnell as one of its own?

14. What does Waterford's Irish name 'Port Láirge' mean?

15. Where was Liam O'Flaherty born?

Specials

answers on page 172

1. Where is Lord Antrim's Parlour?

2. What hard sweet is Ballycastle's Lammas Fair famous for?

3. Who or what were the Palatines?

4. How long was the bridge across Dublin's Royal Canal?

5. Who was the engineer who designed this bridge?

6. What was "a wound which Ireland cannot stanch"?

7. When was Brian Friel born?

8. Why could Brian Friel lay claim to 2 birthdays?

9. How was the Earl of Erne employed from 1855?

10. What was the ILPU?

11. To which O'Brien do we owe the most famous King of the 20th century?

12. What "never came to Ireland until Teilifís Éireann went on the air"?

13. Which Irish rugby players won the VC during the Boer War?

14. What is an 'alickadoo'?

15. What is another name for an 'executive high ball' in rugby?

Specials

answers on page 172

1. When and where was the Orange Order founded?

2. When was New York's first 'St Patrick's Day Parade'?

3. What is taken as the probable date of St Patrick's death?

4. What was notable about Alcock and Brown's landing in Co. Galway?

5. What is the Irish national lottery called?

6. Where did the Irish Brigade meet Pope Pius XII, 12th June 1944?

7. Which wager is James Daly famous for accepting?

8. Which word did James Daly popularise, according to the story?

9. What was James Daly's profession?

10. What was the 'Brendan Voyage'?

11. Who or what are 'na mBráithre Chriostaí'?

12. What were Seventh Heaven and Caveman's Delight?

13. What was opened at Lissadell House in 1925?

14. Daniel O'Donnell is a famous Irishman in which sphere?

15. What planet do Zig and Zag come from?

Sport

answers on page 173

1. How long was John Aldridge's international career?

2. How many Olympic athletics medals had Ireland won before the 2000 Olympics?

3. How many Olympic boxing medals had Ireland won before the 2000 Olympics?

4. How many Olympic swimming medals have Irish men won?

5. According to Jacques McCarthy, sports writer, in which sport do you: 'kick the ball'?

6. What team played against Ireland in its first soccer international?

7. What sport did John Watson take part in?

8. Where was John Watson born?

9. When was John Watson born?

10. What was the highest position John Watson achieved in his sport's Championship?

11. Where was motorcycle ace Joey Dunlop born?

12. When was motorcycle ace Joey Dunlop born?

13. According to Jacques McCarthy, sports writer, in which sport do you: 'kick the man if you cannot kick the ball'?

14. What was the score in Ireland's first soccer international?

15. According to Jacques McCarthy, sports writer, in which sport do you: 'kick the ball if you cannot kick the man'?

Geography

answers on page 173

1. The river Slaney flows through which county?

2. How high are the Cliffs of Moher?

3. Which county has an area of 1764sq km?

4. Which county has an area of 922sq km?

5. On which Donegal island did Napper Tandy land, on 16th September 1798?

6. What specific sort of pilgrimage site could be found near Liscannor, Co. Clare?

7. Where is The Lios?

8. Where was John Philip Holland born?

9. What was "the shortest route between this country and America"?

10. On which Irish island is there definitely a Mermaid?

11. Where is Barntrosna?

12. Lord Mountcharles' estate includes which well-known house?

13. What is another name for the Iveagh Peninsula?

14. Where did the Irish Bards meet until 1746?

15. What does the name Ilnacullin mean?

Sport

answers on page 173

1. In what year did Ireland first win a rugby match at Twickenham?

2. When did motorcycle ace Joey Dunlop die?

3. Which football team did Martin O'Neill sign a contract to manage in June 2000?

4. Which sport do Corinthians play?

5. How many Irish caps did Terry Gregg win?

6. In which sport did Terry Gregg win 103 caps?

7. Which hockey player has captained Ireland, Great Britain and Ulster, winning Olympic Gold and Bronze?

8. What are the Tailteann Games?

9. When were the first 'modern' Tailteann games held?

10. What is the traditional interval between Tailteann games?

11. Which racecourse holds the Irish Champion Stakes?

12. Which horse won the Irish Derby in 1991?

13. Who is the current Northern Ireland football manager?

14. Who did this person replace as Northern Ireland football manager?

15. Who is the current Republic of Ireland football manager?

Geography

answers on page 174

1. Where is The Meeting of the Waters?

2. What is the county town of Tipperary?

3. What is unusual about Mannin Bay in Connemara?

4. Which county has an area of 3263sq km?

5. Which county has an area of 1043sq km?

6. What is the longest river in the British Isles?

7. Which county is also a verse form?

8. Near which lake are the Seven Sisters?

9. Where was Robert Boyle born?

10. Where was the *Victorian*, first turbine-engined vessel to cross the Atlantic, built?

11. From which port did the *Victorian* sail?

12. Which island is named after an ancient Irish sea-god?

13. Where is the Fitzgerald ancestral home?

14. 'The Poisoned Glen' is in which county?

15. Where is the HQ of the Army Air Corps?

Sport

answers on page 174

1. Against which side did footballer Tom Arrigan make his sole international appearance?

2. In which sport is Eddie Irvine a famous participant?

3. Roy Keane is a famous footballer in which two sides?

4. Tony McCoy is a champion in which sport?

5. Which was the last English football team is managed by Martin O'Neill?

6. Who captained Dublin's winning side in 1958?

7. Which team won the senior Hurling championship in 1901?

8. When was the Garda GAA Club founded?

9. Who founded the Garda GAA Club?

10. Why was the Garda GAA Club disbanded?

11. When did the Garda GAA Club reform?

12. Which GAA Army athlete was also an international showjumper?

13. After whom is the Higher Education hurling competition, The Fitzgibbon Cup, named?

14. Which organisation is titled 'Cumann Peile Gael na mBan'?

15. When and where was the Ladies Gaelic Football Association formed?

Geography

answers on page 174

1. Where did WB Yeats die?

2. Which area is continually in dispute between Ireland, Great Britain and Norway?

3. Where is John Greer Dill buried?

4. Which county has an area of 7459sq km?

5. Which county has an area of 1525sq km?

6. Which county has an area of 2352sq km?

7. How long is River Shannon?

8. Name the 3 Aran Islands.

9. Which part of Co. Meath would be home from home to *felix leo*?

10. Ireland lacks snakes, but it does have a Boa Island. Where is it?

11. Where was William McNeven born?

12. In which county is Lough Ahalia?

13. Lugnaquilla is the highest mountain in which county?

14. Where was Francis Johnston born, in 1760?

15. Where was actor Aidan Quinn born?

Geography

answers on page 174

1. The Lake of Killarney was once known as?

2. Which county has an area of 635sq km?

3. Which county has an area of 1694sq km?

4. In which city did Daniel O'Connell die?

5. Which Cavan town was famous for its spa waters?

6. In which county is Lissyviggeen?

7. Where is Mount Cairnbone?

8. What stands on the northern shore of Lake Tacumshane?

9. Which Irish bay sounds as if it has named after a French writer?

10. What was the Lagan Navigation?

11. Where would you find Hare's Castle?

12. What connects the Carrick-a-rede rock with the rest of the island?

13. In which city was The Messiah first performed?

14. Which northern Irish town styles itself the 'city of the seven towers', although it possesses no cathedral?

15. In which county are the Caha mountains?

Specials

answers on page 175

1. Juno (as *Juno and the Paycock*) is the wife of which Roman god?

2. How was Lough Neagh created, according to legend?

3. What is St Patrick said to have done in Black Lough, the Gap of Dunloe?

4. How long did the enchantment of the Children of Lir last?

5. What were the names of the Children of Lir?

6. How many Senators sat in Stormont?

7. What is the significance of the butterfly in Irish folklore?

8. What was 'gavelkind'?

9. What was Cuchulainn's 'Gae-Bolg'?

10. What were Cuchulainn's horses called?

11. What was Cuchulainn's father-in-law called?

12. Which Irish mythological figure is the equivalent of Gawain's Green Knight?

13. What was his challenge to Cuchulainn?

14. Who or what is Lurigethan?

15. Who said "What is the stars"?

Geography

answers on page 175

1. Lough Gealain lies within which spectacular area?

2. Where do 'the mountains of Mourne sweep down to the sea'?

3. Which county has an area of 3100sq km?

4. Which county has an area of 2686sq km?

5. Which county has an area of 5397sq km?

6. Which saint has an island named after them in Templeport Lake, in Co. Cavan?

7. What do the names of the Aran Islands mean in English?

8. Which is the 'metropolitan' county of Ireland?

9. Which body of water may be found near The Lios?

10. What ancient monuments can be found on Mount Cairnbone?

11. What item of interest might you find on Mount Browne, Carlow?

12. Where were the first 'Irish' Puritans to be found?

13. Where would you be if you thought 'the girls are so pretty'?

14. On which river does Cork stand?

15. Which island off Co. Cork is also known as Ilnacullin?

Specials

answers on page 175

1. Which formula one motor racing team is headed by an Irishman?

2. What did St Brigid famously use to gain land for her religious community?

3. What was unusual about St Brigid's clothing?

4. Which county does Peter Canavan represent in gaelic games?

5. Which Irish aristocrat was Viceroy of India and Governor General of Canada in the 1880s and '90s?

6. What is another name for the Priory of Lough Derg?

7. How many people made the journey from Belfast to Lisburn by rail on the Ulster Railway's first day in 1836?

8. 'Phelim Brady, the Bard of Armagh' held another office. What was it?

9. What memento of St Patrick did Red Island in Co. Dublin retain?

10. Drumragh and Camowen rivers join to form which other river near Omagh?

11. Who attacked the fishing town of Baltimore in Co. Cork in the 17th century, carrying away people to slavery in Africa?

12. Who landed in Co. Galway on 15th June 1919?

13. Who said 'from the graves of patriot men and women spring living nations'?

14. Who wrote 'Like crows attacking crow-black fields, they stretch'?

15. In which language was Samuel Beckett's poem *Poem* written?

Geography

answers on page 176

1. Bunclody in Co. Wicklow has another name. What is it?

2. What is Ireland's smallest county?

3. Where did William Rowan Hamilton live from age 22 to his death?

4. Where was Ernest Walton born?

5. St. Fergal was bishop of which city?

6. Where is the National Maritime Museum?

7. Complete the title of this Oliver Goldsmith work - *Citizen of...*?

8. What now stands on the former site of the 'Causeway Safari Park'?

9. Which city is the subject of the ballad *The Bells of Shandon*?

10. Who wrote 'The groves of Blarney/ They look so charming'?

11. Where did the Ulster Canal originate?

12. The Spelga Pass links which towns?

13. Who was the nineteenth-century 'uncrowned King of Ireland'?

14. What were transmitted and received from 16 October 1907, at Clifden in Galway?

15. What is Armagh Observatory commonly known as?

Geography
(page 4)

1. Slieve Gamph
2. Limerick
3. Fergus and Shannon
4. On Lough Gill in Co. Sligo
5. Black Head
6. Lough Corrib
7. Lough Mask
8. 40,000
9. Basalt
10. 6
11. 26
12. Donegal
13. Eels
14. The Liffey
15. Armagh, Cavan, Coleraine, Donegal, Fermanagh, Tyrone

History
(page 5)

1. Lambert Simnel, 1487
2. Thurgesius
3. Lia fail (the Stone of Destiny, which was transported to Scotland)
4. Merrion Street, Dublin
5. 1845-49
6. First of July 1690
7. The 1641 Catholic Rebellion
8. Dunseverick Castle
9. Henry Joy McCracken
10. The United Irishmen
11. Norsemen, vikings
12. 1925, between the governments of Northern Ireland, Eire, Great Britain
13. Brehon law
14. John Mitchel
15. Sir Walter Raleigh

Sport
(page 6)

1. Coalisland
2. Football (soccer)
3. Hurling
4. Pentathlon
5. Tipperary beat Galway by 1 goal & 1 point to 0
6. The Gaelic Athletic Association for the Preservation and Cultivation of our national Pastimes
7. PJ Prendergast
8. Billiards
9. The billiard-room of Miss Hayes's Commercial Hotel in Thurles
10. Ireland and USA
11. Hockey
12. Leeds United
13. Thomond Park
14. Galway, Kerry, Offaly and Tipperary
15. Deliberate bodily contact

Politics
(page 7)

1. 1264
2. Hurling
3. James Connolly
4. Irish senator
5. Theobald Wolfe Tone
6. Sean MacBride

7. An tÓglach
8. Constance Markiewicz, 28th December 1918
9. She declined to sit in the British parliament
10. 17th January 1860
11. Ivory Coast (Côte d'Ivoire)
12. Henry Grattan
13. New York
14. The Speaker of the Irish Parliament
15. Thomas Brady, 1752-1857

Literature   *(page 8)*

1. Roddy Doyle
2. *'Tis*
3. *The Primrose Path*
4. *Paddy Clarke Ha Ha Ha*
5. February 2nd, 1882
6. February 2nd, 1922
7. Edmund Burke
8. *Stephen Hero*
9. Louis MacNeice
10. From the hide of the animal on which the text was written
11. Snake venom (possibly because of the link to St Patrick)
12. Clive Staples Lewis
13. Cuchulainn
14. The Gospels
15. *Lamb*

Irish Language   *(page 9)*

1. The Cattle Raid of Cooley
2. High King of Ireland
3. Monday
4. May
5. Rugbaí
6. Long
7. Ring
8. It stresses and stretches the sound
9. Irish Parliament
10. A poet, an historian
11. The hedgehog
12. An animal-skin boat from Co. Kerry
13. Irish Mountaineering Club
14. Dark stranger, 'dubh' black, 'gall' stranger
15. Irish whiskey

Music   *(page 10)*

1. Andrew Strong
2. The N17
3. The flute
4. It was made of gold
5. Midge Ure
6. July 13, 1985
7. St Michan's, Dublin
8. Limavady, Co. Derry
9. *Danny Boy*
10. Abide With Me
11. Gerald Barry
12. Co. Clare, 1952
13. Tenor
14. Terry Woods
15. Neil Hannon

People (page 11)

1. C. Day Lewis, of Constance Markiewicz
2. West Britons
3. John Ford, *The Quiet Man*
4. O'Connell of Derrinane Abbey, Co. Kerry
5. Daniel O'Connell
6. 'Ciall agus ceart'
7. Right and strength
8. 'Invitum sequitur honor'
9. Honour follows though unsought for
10. Veterinary Surgeon
11. He calculated the date of Creation, from Biblical information
12. 3rd Earl of Rosse
13. Ireland's Eye
14. Thomas Stucley, 16th c. adventurer
15. Captain Bligh, notorious captain of the *Bounty*

Personalities (page 12)

1. GB Shaw's work was described as being "marked by both idealism and humanity."
2. James Joyce
3. Nora Barnacle
4. Amelia Earhart
5. William Henry O'Shea and Katherine (Kitty) O'Shea
6. Andrew Browne Cunningham, 1st Viscount Cunningham of Hyndhope
7. He was a Belfast linen manufacturer
8. John Mitchel
9. John Mitchel
10. Jeremiah
11. Ellen Hanley
12. Speranza
13. An Irishman competing in the first modern Olympics
14. Jerome O'Shea, Kerry goalie of the 1950s
15. As the real name of Maureen O'Hara

Poetry (page 13)

1. Derry
2. WB Yeats
3. Physical harm against the listener it was aimed at
4. 28th January 1939
5. Samuel Ferguson
6. William McBurney
7. Lady Wilde
8. Lady Wilde, 'The Famine Year'
9. Padraig Pearse
10. Francis Ledwidge
11. William Drennan
12. 'No, it is not'
13. Louis MacNeice
14. Jonathan Swift
15. Art O'Leary

Specials (page 14)

1. The gift of the gab
2. Island off the coast of Mayo
3. A town or townland near New Ross
4. 3
5. Jonathan Swift
6. Munster

7. Because he died on January 13th 1941
8. A Scottish soldier who fought in Ireland; 'foreign warrior' in Irish is 'gall óglach'
9. Man-made islands on which wooden fortifications were built
10. Cuchulainn
11. Trinity College, Dublin, founded 1592
12. Formal education for Catholics was prevented by Penal Laws: children were taught in fields at any opportunity
13. His heart, which was left in the Church of St Agatha in Rome
14. A riotous assembly, an all-in fight
15. A fair held in Donnybrook, Dublin

Literature   *(page 15)*

1. *The Book of the Dun Cow*
2. 300, according to annals of Clonmacnois
3. Tara
4. O'Clery
5. Michael O'Clery
6. No. 7, Eccles Street, Dublin
7. Arthur Joyce Lunel Carey
8. *Murphy*
9. William Trevor
10. May 24, 1928
11. Flann O'Brien
12. Somerville and Ross
13. Martin
14. Sean O'Faolain
15. *The Sea, The Sea*

Geography   *(page 16)*

1. On a beach at Bettystown, Drogheda
2. Tara, Co. Meath
3. Leix (now Laois)
4. Achill Island
5. Ossian's Grave, on Tievebulliagh, nr Cushendall in Co. Antrim
6. It had an ancient church made of sandstone in a county of predominantly limestone
7. Maelruan's Plague Grave
8. Rock of Cashel - the devil took a bite from a mountain, but spat it into the sea
9. Roscommon
10. Monaghan
11. Sligo
12. Cavan, Donegal and Monaghan
13. Birr, Co. Offaly
14. Carlow
15. Belvedere, Co. Westmeath

History   *(page 17)*

1. Blarney Castle
2. Dublin and Anagassan (between Dundalk and Drogheda
3. 807 AD
4. Fines
5. *c.* 840AD
6. From Borinne, nr. Killaloe, Co Clare
7. Brian Boru
8. 1002
9. Clontarf
10. Clontarf, 1014
11. Waterford
12. 1607
13. Aughrim
14. Commanche, horse of Myles Keogh, Irish soldier who fought with Custer
15. John Barry

Irish Language   (page 18)

1. A 'beehive' stone structure
2. The Arts Council of Ireland
3. Wednesday
4. Thursday
5. February
6. July
7. November
8. It is a pin which shows the wearer's ease in Irish
9. Green
10. Eat it - it's a mutton broth
11. A potato and cabbage dish
12. The robin
13. Kells
14. Irish Language Board, promoting the use of the Irish language
15. Heron

Music   (page 19)

1. George Ivan Morrison
2. 1982
3. The Rising of the Moon
4. 1977
5. *Chinatown*
6. Leo's Tavern, Gweedore, Donegal
7. Leo Brennan, father to members of group
8. Co. Meath, 1850
9. The Cranberries
10. Slane
11. Rosemary Brown
12. Bill Whelan
13. Margaret Burke Sheridan
14. Peadar Kearney, 1883-1942
15. Guitar based blues

People   (page 20)

1. Edinburgh, Scotland
2. 'little fawn', from the Celtic
3. Royal poet ('riogh' royal, 'bardán', poet, bard)
4. Miss Nano Nagle
5. Bishop of Cloyne
6. Earl of Cork and Orrery
7. 'Ginger'
8. Columbanus
9. Easter
10. Arland Ussher, 1949
11. A leader of workers' strikes and Union organisation
12. Cathedral of St. Mary's (Roman Catholic)
13. George Freidrich Handel, the composer
14. Lord Thomas FitzGerald, in the 16th century
15. James Louis O'Donnell

Personalities   (page 21)

1. Bram Stoker
2. Louis MacNeice
3. 14
4. Daniel Day-Lewis
5. St Malachy, bishop of Armagh
6. Robert Emmet

7. Daniel O'Connell
8. Sir Robert Peel, chief secretary to Ireland
9. Padraig Pearse
10. 3
11. 3rd Marquis of Londonderry, 1851
12. The deceased king Brian Boru and his dead son Murrough, after the Battle of Clontarf
13. Tom Crean
14. Constance Markiewicz
15. Charles Haughey, 13th August 1982

Poetry (page 22)

1. WB Yeats
2. *The Croppy Boy*
3. JM Synge
4. Thomas McDonough
5. Oliver St John Gogarty
6. Oliver Goldsmith
7. Poem
8. Louis MacNeice
9. *The Village*
10. Oliver Goldsmith
11. *Stella's Birthday*
12. English
13. 8th century
14. Irish
15. 13th April 1939

Specials (page 23)

1. Greyhounds
2. Tyrone (as in Tyrone Power)
3. 16th June
4. A disfigured person was considered ineligible for election as king or chief
5. An area around Dublin, into Leinster
6. Irish landowners
7. It was settled by Cromwell's forces
8. It is the Latin term for 'potato blight'
9. 1850
10. Queen's Colleges of Galway, Cork and Belfast
11. The Queen's University
12. A double-peaked islet with a lighthouse along Ireland's south coast
13. *Endurance*
14. An optical illusion makes it appear that objects run uphill, contrary to gravity
15. A shroud or winding-sheet

Sport (page 24)

1. Dublin University, in 1854
2. 20
3. Barry McGuigan
4. Mallow, Co. Cork, 1752
5. Horses raced between 2 church spires (steeples)
6. It was unfinished, due to USA invasion by GAA athletes
7. 1864
8. Lory Meagher
9. Liam and Ronnie Whelan, 1957 and 1964 against England
10. Arsenal
11. Australian Rules Football
12. Bicycle Polo
13. Croke Park
14. 12-0
15. Boxing

Politics   *(page 25)*

1. Clare
2. Lord Randolph Churchill, in 1886
3. 6th July 1946
4. 30th May 1973
5. 7th November 1974
6. Sean T. O'Kelly
7. United Nations
8. 7 years
9. Daniel O'Connell
10. William Ferguson Massey - Massey Ferguson is a tractor manufacturer
11. Round room of Dublin's Mansion House
12. 21st January 1919
13. Prime Minister of Northern Ireland
14. Pope Pius X, 27th April 1905
15. National Socialist League

Geography   *(page 26)*

1. Co. Cork
2. 32
3. In Co.Galway, near Thoor Ballylee
4. Rathmullen, Lough Swilly, Co. Donegal
5. Scotland
6. 4 (Ulster, Munster, Leinster, Connacht)
7. Dinn Rig, on the river Barrow
8. Londonderry/ Derry
9. 2796 feet
10. Kilronan church, Lough Meelagh, Co. Roscommon
11. In the Slieve Bloom range
12. Carrantuohill, Beenkeragh and Caher (3414, 3314, 3200 feet)
13. Station Island
14. Carrick-on-Shannon
15. Clones, Co. Monaghan

History   *(page 27)*

1. The Duke of Wellington
2. 14th September, 1607
3. Lord of Ireland
4. 15th August 1649
5. 7th December 1688
6. 13
7. 28th July 1689
8. While fighting for France against William of Orange at the battle of Landen, Flanders
9. Castles built from1429 in the Pale area of Ireland, with £10 grant from government
10. 25 minutes behind Greenwich
11. 20 feet in length 16 feet in width and 40 feet in height or more
12. 105 days
13. English and Spanish navies
14. Hugh de Lacy
15. *Victorian*

People   *(page 28)*

1. Queen's University Belfast
2. Queen Victoria
3. United States of America
4. Milchu
5. Laurence - his descendants were Baronets
6. "part of it I know to be false, another part I believe not to be true"

7. Norman settlers of Welsh and Flemish origin
8. Michelle de Bruin
9. 1st January 1730
10. Catherine McAuley
11. St Brigid
12. Gore-Booth
13. A French general on the side of King James, 1691
14. Mick Doyle
15. St Laurence O'Toole

Specials   *(page 29)*

1. Blinding by needle
2. She was strangled (or drowned in the Shannon) at her husband John Scanlan's orders, in 1819
3. Its ruddy (red-tinged) sunsets
4. Mountains in Co. Waterford
5. The Irish Sea - Scots 'gallic' and Irish 'gaelic'
6. Danu
7. Arthur Guinness
8. Wrens
9. Certificates of pardon for surrendering United Irishmen, signed by Lord Cornwallis
10. Irish MPs in the British House of Commons
11. Dramatist
12. Conan, the barbarian, because conan ('ceannann' in Irish) means bald
13. An ancient stone circle
14. Royal Society for the Prevention of Cruelty to Animals
15. Tobacco

Sport   *(page 30)*

1. Irish Rugby Football Union
2. Joshua Pim, 1893
3. 1926
4. Arsenal, Leeds
5. 1952, Silver medal
6. 1956
7. 1956
8. Bantamweight and Lightweight
9. Welterweight
10. Tennis singles, and doubles with a German
11. Jaguar
12. Handball
13. The RIC
14. Only man ever to win both All-Ireland medal (gaelic football) and FA Cup medal (Manchester Unuted)
15. Twice GAA (1976-77) FA (1983, 85)

Politics   *(page 31)*

1. Dublin University
2. John O'Mahony
3. Mary Harney and Des O'Malley
4. 8
5. Home Rule for Ireland
6. 72 days
7. Fianna Fail
8. 'Soldiers of Destiny'
9. William Gladstone
10. Mary McAleese
11. Derry City and the National University of Ireland
12. 'Tribe of the Gaels'
13. Gerry Fitt, later Lord Fitt
14. Eamon de Valera
15. Mary

Geography   *(page 32)*

1. Isle of Man, in the Irish Sea
2. Skreen, Co. Sligo
3. Commercial fishing
4. Co. Kildare
5. Lucerne, Switzerland
6. The Small Weir
7. Kingstown
8. Avondale, Co. Wicklow
9. Fenit, near Tralee, in 483AD
10. Brandon Mountain, Kerry, 3127 feet
11. Roscommon
12. Connemara
13. Roscommon
14. Cork
15. Laois/ Leix

History   *(page 33)*

1. General Humbert, of France
2. Protestant 'Peep O'Day Boys', and Catholic 'Defenders'
3. St. Columbkille's Well (sórd means 'well')
4. 1902
5. Earl of Lucan
6. Any man with an unshaven upper lip
7. The Black Death
8. 'of an ulcer, which had broken out on his foot'
9. The province of Ulster
10. A Provisional Government
11. The area around Killala, Connaught in 1798
12. John Moore
13. Maurice Fitzgerald
14. 3rd January 1946 in London
15. Francis Stuart

Irish Language   *(page 34)*

1. Tuesday
2. Friday
3. January
4. March
5. Fada
6. Peile Gaelach
7. A hurling ball
8. Teachta Dála, member of Irish parliament
9. Irish House of Representatives
10. A storyteller or bard
11. White
12. The Irish Tourist Board
13. An expanse of grass on which fairs and gatherings took place
14. Freedom
15. An early Irish team ball-game

Music   *(page 35)*

1. Guitar and harmonica
2. RTÉ Radio 2
3. Band Aid/ Live Aid
4. Bono Vox
5. From a sign advertising a hearing aid - 'Bono Vox'
6. 40

*7. Turlough O'Carolan
8. *New York*
9. 'Póg mo' means 'kiss my' in Irish, 'hoan' refers to the posterior
10. Shane MacGowan
11. Abul Abulbul Ameer
12. Richard Brinsley Sheridan
13. Paul Hewson
14. The Popes
15. Christopher Davidson

People (page 36)

1. Hurricane
2. Theobald
3. Richard de Burgo, a Norman
4. Presentation Order
5. 'I hope what I shall be'
6. 21.30%
7. 1859
8. James Larkin
9. Oliver J. Flanagan, Fine Gael TD, March 1966
10. A nun who worked in the hospital, 20th March 1964, where he died
11. Marjorie
12. Pirate Queen
13. Francis Johnston
14. Baron von Hunefield, Captain Koehl, Colonel Fitzmaurice
15. The 'Liberator of Chile'

Poetry (page 37)

1. *The Deer's Cry*
2. Seamus Justin Heaney
3. Rudyard Kipling
4. Brian Merriman
5. Henry Brooke
6. *An Irish Airman Foresees His Death*
7. WB Yeats
8. 'clay and wattles'
9. *Down By The Salley Gardens*
10. *September 1913* by WB Yeats
11. Gerard Manley Hopkins
12. Francis Sylvester O'Mahony
13. *September 1913*
14. Edmund Spenser
15. Irish

Specials (page 38)

1. 1962
2. The main character in Joyce' *Ulysses*, Leopold Bloom, begins his odyssey through Dublin on this date
3. Finn MacCool
4. Catholic religious services were curtailed, so Mass was said in out-of-the-way fields, using rocks as altars
5. Skellig-Michael
6. 'grotesque, unprecedented, bizarre and unique'
7. West of Clonakilty Bay, Cork
8. Woodstock
9. As part of an ill-advised extension programme - too much gunpowder was used
10. The punt
11. A cannon in Derry during its long siege
12. A small island north of Howth in Co. Dublin
13. Motor racing and motorcycle circuit
14. Dulse and yellow man
15. Shantemon Hill, Cavan, Co. Cavan

Sport *(page 39)*

1. Wanderers and Lansdowne
2. Toomebridge, Co. Antrim
3. Willie John McBride
4. Arsenal, Derby county, Blackburn rovers, Huddersfield town, Bradford City
5. Golf
6. He forgot to sign his tournament score card, invalidating his play
7. Ruby Walsh
8. Papillon
9. Ted Walsh
10. Father and son
11. They were both trained and ridden by father-son teams
12. Winner won Grand National in 1999, runner-up won Grand National in 2000
13. Leeds United
14. Bobbyjo
15. Hammer-throw

Politics *(page 40)*

1. Chaim Herzog
2. 2nd January 1986
3. Frenchpark, Co. Roscommon
4. 2
5. Many people signed in their own blood
6. Eamon de Valera, Irish mother, Spanish father
7. 35 years
8. 3
9. Mary Banotti
10. 'Warriors of Destiny'
11. Dublin Castle
12. Michael Collins, 18th August 1922
13. 22nd August 1922, in an ambush by his 'own countrymen'
14. JH Thomas, Dominions Secretary, 1931
15. UUP

Literature *(page 41)*

1. The Red Branch Cycle
2. Latin
3. Brendan Behan
4. Vampires
5. 1904
6. Jonathan Swift
7. At Swim-Two Birds
8. Irish Murdoch
9. Jonathan Swift
10. Munster, in the 18th century
11. Drogheda
12. Chapelizod
13. Anne McCaffrey
14. Flann O'Brien
15. Violet Martin (Ross from her home, Ross House)

Industry *(page 42)*

1. Music
2. They opened the first cinema in Dublin, the Volta
3. 19 days
4. John R. Gregg
5. Linen
6. Potato crisps

7. Dr. John Colohon, of Blackrock, Co. Dublin
8. A bubble car produced under license in Co. Down
9. John Boyd Dunlop
10. The Russian government's first steam ice-breaker
11. Avoca
12. *Olympic*
13. Harland & Wolff
14. *Brittanic, Olympic, Titanic*
15. 46,000 tons

Films   (page 43)

1. *The Commitments*
2. *Pulp Fiction*
3. *Star Wars: Episode One*
4. *Darkman*
5. *Evita*, directed by Alan Parker
6. *Nora*
7. *Excalibur* and *Star Wars: Episode One*
8. *An American Werewolf in London*
9. Ardmore Studios
10. *Into The West*
11. *The Usual Suspects*
12. *Stigmata* and *End of Days* as, respectively a priest and the Devil
13. *Braveheart*
14. *Fahrenheit 451*
15. Maureen O'Sullivan

Geography   (page 44)

1. Dublin (named after a real street)
2. Rathlin Island
3. Lagan
4. Northern Ireland
5. Donegal
6. 5
7. Temuir, better known as Tara
8. In the north of Co. Antrim
9. New York
10. Glenarm, Glenaan, Glenariff
11. Slieveardagh Hills
12. Killyleagh, Co. Down
13. Mainwater
14. Royal acropolis
15. Villierstown, Co. Waterford

History   (page 45)

1. He slit his own throat in prison
2. There is always more than one 'winner'
3. Erskine Childers
4. The George Cross, for valour
5. United States
6. Sir James Fitzmaurice
7. Pope Gregory XIII
8. Monday 24th April 1916
9. Colonel Thomas Blood, 1618-80
10. Edward Bruce
11. Belfast
12. 12th August 1922
13. 9th August 1922
14. 1883, between Portrush and Bushmills, Co. Antrim
15. William Burke, Cork (Burke and Hare)

Irish Language *(page 46)*

1. Sunday
2. April
3. September
4. December
5. Iománaíocht
6. A hurley stick
7. Irish Senate
8. Blue
9. Fairy folk (pronounced 'shee')
10. An Irish folk group
11. The Cathedral of Derry
12. 'Ireland for ever'
13. Fia
14. 'Sean Bhean Vocht' or 'poor old woman' - Ireland in the 19th century
15. Capall

Music *(page 47)*

1. Dante Alighieri
2. Owen Roe O'Neill (1590-1649)
3. Thomas Osborne Davis (1814-45)
4. 7th January 1965
5. 'sweep down to the sea'
6. Bono, Edge, Adam Clayton, Larry Mullen
7. Adam Clayton
8. Boyzone, B*witched, Buffalo G
9. Westlife
10. Mother Bernadette Mary
11. Christy Moore
12. *The Banished Defender*
13. *My Lovely Horse*
14. Chris de Burgh
15. Belfast

People *(page 48)*

1. Sean MacBride
2. He was a poet
3. The Sugane Earl
4. John Scanlan's murder of his wife, 'The Colleen Bawn'
5. Their fame - as motorcycle racers, they depend on the pneumatic tyre, invented by Dunlop
6. She was James Joyce's benefactor, supporting his writing with funds
7. Daniel O'Connell
8. Sir John D. Cockcroft
9. Kitty Kiernan
10. Gromwell, Hillsborough, Co. Down
11. Edmund Ignatius Rice
12. Church of Ireland
13. The Countess of Desart, 1881
14. Kilkenny Woollen Mills
15. Shiny Entertainment

Personalities *(page 49)*

1. CS Lewis
2. James
3. Turlough O'Carolan
4. Accounts vary between 110 and 162 years of age
5. Annascaul, Co. Kerry
6. Edward Bansfield, born in Cork in 1783
7. Admiral of the Fleet (Royal Navy)

8. Esperanto
9. Setanta
10. Edward Joshua Cooper (1798-1863)
11. Ernest Thomas Sinton Walton
12. Lucasian Professor of Mathematics, Cambridge University
13. 1747-1805
14. WB Yeats
15. Constance Markiewicz

Religion *(page 50)*

1. Saint Patrick
2. Bishop Palladius
3. The Navigator
4. Daniel Mannix, of Charleville
5. A fragment of 'the true Cross'
6. Bedell, in the 17th century
7. The Knights Templar
8. Pope Alexander VI, 1497
9. Ruadhan of Lorrha
10. The Ark of the Covenant
11. 16th May
12. 'Wolves'. In 1650, an anti-clerical syllogism (a piece of subtle, deceptive reasoning) ran:
'priests are the cause of all Ireland's woes; wolves are a misery; therefore priests are to blame for the existence of wolves'
13. 784AD
14. 1184
15. 13th April 1742

Specials *(page 51)*

1. Scallions, spring onions
2. A mixture of Irish whiskey and honey
3. A celebration of the life of the deceased
4. World Heritage Site
5. 2 metres higher and 10m larger in diameter
6. Off Dursey Head (they are islets)
7. Keeper of Loop Head lighthouse
8. A Cork naval base, completed in 1894
9. A Co. Down fishing vessel
10. The anemometer
11. It was the first vessel to carry the Irish tricolour around the world
12. Sir Edward Carson
13. He successfully prosecuted Oscar Wilde, and was involved as defence counsel in the case brought to the theatre by playwright Terence Rattigan as 'The Winslow Boy'
14. The first artificial salmon river
15. First maternity hospital in Great Britain or Ireland, 1757

Sport *(page 52)*

1. 1500 metres
2. 1996
3. Jimmy White, 1928 against Belgium
4. Arsenal, Tottenham Hotspur, Watford
5. 1
6. Tommy and Paul Carberry
7. He was champion amateur jockey 11 times
8. The Grand National
9. Bowls
10. 'Tiger' Woods
11. San Jose Earthquakes
120 He rode 253 winners in a riding season
13. City West
14. It is the 2nd oldest rugby club in the world
15. 1854

ANSWERS

Television (page 53)

1. 12th April 1960
2. Divis Mountain, Belfast
3. The Late Late Show
4. Gay Byrne
5. Pat Kenny
6. *Catchphrase*
7. 'Say what you see'
8. Zig and Zag
9. Turkey
10. Vale of Avoca, Co. Wicklow
11. Fitzgerald's
12. Assumpta Fitzgerald
13. Builder
14. Terry Wogan
15. 1962

Natural History (page 54)

1. University College, Cork - Fota Wildlife Park is on land still owned by the University.
2. George Johnstone Stoney, 1826-1911, Irish physicist
3. Theory of quaternions, 3 dimensional calculus
4. Astronomer Royal of Ireland
5. George Boole, of 'Boolean algebra' fame
6. Dillisk
7. James Ussher, Archbishop of Armagh
8. William McNeven, 1763-1841
9. 6000x
10. President of the Royal Society
11. Charles Parsons (1854-1931) invented the steam turbine
12. His seventh son, Robert Boyle, was called 'the father of chemistry'
13. John Brinkley, in 1792
14. Humphrey Lloyd, 1800-81
15. 1830

History (page 55)

1. 'Orange Peel'
2. 22nd March 1969
3. Fine Gael
4. 12th July 1949
5. Human Rights
6. James Craig
7. Arthur Griffith
8. Benjamin Disraeli, British Prime Minister
9. 1886
10. Michael Collins
11. In Belfast, 1918
12. SDLP
13. Ulster Unionist Party
14. Isaac Butt
15. Jack Lynch (1917-1999)

Arts (page 56)

1. *The Egoist*
2. Percy French
3. 590AD, at the Convention of All Ireland at Drumceat
4. Cape Breton, Canada
5. Belfast's *News Letter*
6. *The Derry Journal*

7. *The Impartial Reporter*
8. 'Oldie of the Year'
9. Thomas Davis
10. Dublin
11. His 'Screaming Popes', variations on a papal portrait by Velasquez
12. Isabella Augusta Gregory
13. *Skibbereen Eagle*
14. 'The largest penny paper in the world'
15. *The Southern Star*

Geography   (page 57)

1. Cork, Galway, Dublin
2. Cong
3. Nine
4. Cork, Limerick and Dublin
5. Wales
6. Leinster (from North Leinster and South Leinster)
7. Slieve Donard
8. Antrim
9. Glentaisie, Glenshesk, Glencloy
10. Killiney
11. Old Head of Kinsale
12. River Maine
13. Castlebar
14. Longford
15. Carlow

History   (page 58)

1. 1783
2. Don Juan d'Aguila, having occupied the town
3. Charles Thompson
4. 36th Ulster Division
5. The elder Childers was executed as a Republican in the Civil War, the younger later became President of Ireland
6. It is now a museum dedicated to Pearse
7. Amiens Street
8. Robert the Bruce, of Scotland
9. 1814, as Peace Preservation Police, 15 years before the London force
10. Tuesday 16th April 1782
11. Free State
12. Former Secretary of State for Northern Ireland, Mo Mowlam, September 1999
13. 1947
14. 1969
15. 1902

Music   (page 59)

1. Paris (*Parisian Walkways*)
2. Portstewart, Co. Derry, in the beautiful north
3. Joseph Campbell
4. Derry, Aughrim, Enniskillen and the Boyne
5. David Evans
6. *Nothing Compares 2 U*
7. Barry Moore
8. Josef Locke
9. Jack Donohue, 'Jack Duggan' in song
10. Castlemaine, Kerry, 1809
11. *A Spaceman came Travelling*
12. Westside
13. *All Kinds of Everything*
14. 'Father Prout'
15. The Chieftains

People

(page 60)

1. Nora Barnacle, James Joyce's wife
2. Maud Gonne (MacBride)
3. Monarch of Ireland, 616-628 AD
4. Thomas D'Arcy McGee, 1825-68
5. Inventing a workable submarine
6. A boxer, born 1788
7. John Greer Dill, World War II Field Marshal
8. American
9. Seamus Heaney
10. Admiral of the Fleet, Earl Beatty
11. The first Mass on Australian soil. He was a Catholic priest
12. The first ever Victoria Cross
13. Eva
14. John de Courcy
15. 'Boy'

Specials

(page 61)

1. 18th century English militias in Ireland
2. The Irish tricolour
3. Carrigeen moss
4. A telescope
5. A lightship, to warn of dangerous waters
6. After John Pidgeon, caretaker of works on the South Wall
7. A fishing boat
8. James Stephens, Fenian leader, writing in 1862
9. Erskine Childers snr.
10. Childers made daring seaplane raids against German forces in 1914-16
11. Doohulla or Emlaghmore fishery
12. Galway loughs
13. The by-product of burning seaweed
14. The Academy Award
15. A variation on the sport of handball

Sport

(page 62)

1. Melbourne, Australia, 1956
2. 4 (3 gold, 1 bronze)
3. Munster and the Ireland side
4. No one - it was declared 'no result' due to travel complications - the Troubles
5. Joe Golding
6. Tom Arrigan
7. Peter O'Donohoe of Cavan
8. 2 Gold
9. 1, Silver
10. 27
11. Trinity
12. The first road race to be won at over 60 mph
13. Hubert Hassall
14. Motorcycles
15. 3

Politics

(page 63)

1. 10th March 1987
2. Lord Craigavon
3. W.T. Cosgrave
4. Women's Coalition
5. State Attorney for New York
6. August 1970

7. Constance Markiewicz
8. Irish Unionist Alliance
9. John Hume and David Trimble
10. Social Democratic and Labour Party
11. DUP
12. 1927
13. Michael Collins
14. North Antrim
15. Father Michael O'Flanagan (1876-1942)

Literature   (page 64)

1. Roddy Doyle
2. Michael Davitt
3. James Joyce
4. Novelist John Banim
5. Irish priests
6. Mitchelstown, County Cork
7. Short story writer Frank O'Connor
8. Edith
9. 1833
10. Dublin
11. Bernard McLaverty
12. Clonmel, Co. Tipperary
13. Christopher Nolan
14. Myles na Gopaleen (another pseudonym)
15. Old Gaelic poems and sagas

Industry   (page 65)

1. Computer software
2. Zero
3. Parian china
4. Massey-Ferguson
5. The De Lorean Motor Company
6. The metal bodywork was not painted
7. Benz Viktoria, bought in 1896
8. Tractor
9. Henry Ford (whose grandfather was Irish)
10. Short Bros. & Harland Ltd.
11. Chambers Motors Ltd of Belfast
12. Scottish
13. 1857
14. Herring
15. Hillsborough, Co. Down, 31st December 1909

Films   (page 66)

1. *The General*
2. It was shot in black and white.
3. *Them*
4. *Odd Man Out*
5. *The Informer*
6. Milo O'Shea
7. Stephen Boyd
8. *Fantastic Voyage*
9. *Back To The Future*, Parts 1-3
10. 88 miles per hour
11. Robert Flaherty
12. Screenplay
13. 1928 (the first year of the Awards)
14. *Mrs Miniver*
15. Sean Thornton

ANSWERS

Geography (page 67)

1. Temuir Erann, near Ardpatrick, Limerick
2. Glencorp, Glenballyemon, Glendun
3. Waterford
4. Wexford
5. Cavan
6. Lord Kelvin was born in Belfast
7. Kerry
8. Kilkenny
9. 17 miles long by 11 miles wide
10. Wexford harbour
11. The Burren, a remark made by one of Oliver Cromwell's officers
12. Dublin's Royal Hospital at Kilmainham
13. Dalkey, Co. Dublin
14. Tipperary
15. Roscommon

History (page 68)

1. In 1609, with a charter from King James I
2. 1601
3. 'Murder'
4. 12th March 1689, at Kinsale
5. July 1803
6. Robert Emmet
7. 15th August, 1843
8. In 1848, year of European revolution
9. John Mitchel
10. His refusal to sell his horse for £5
11. A Penal Law restricted Catholics to owning horses worth less than £5
12. 19th November 1798
13. Dublin on 20th June 1763
14. An Irish secret society
15. Kinsale

Irish Language (page 69)

1. Saturday
2. June
3. August
4. October
5. Enda, with Edna
6. Orange
7. Red
8. Pig's feet, seen by some as edible
9. The Irish Turf/ Coal Board
10. *The Sword of Light*, a newspaper of the Gaelic League
11. Woman of the fairy (bean-sidhe)
12. Réadlann
13. 'Inis Badhbha', Island of the War Goddess
14. 'Water of Life'
15. An ancient female fertility symbol

Music (page 70)

1. Garryowen
2. On the bridge of Toome, Toomebridge, Co. Antrim
3. Mary O'Hara
4. U2
5. Temple High School in Dublin
6. Latin Tridentine

7. Moving Hearts and Planxty
8. Val Doonican
9. Argentina, in 1948
10. *Barry Lyndon*
11. 1995
12. Piano
13. Chris de Burgh
14. Boyzone
15. 1994 - with *Rock and Roll Kids*

People   (page 71)

1. William Butler Yeats
2. Thomas Davis
3. Carolan, the blind harper
4. Oscar Wilde
5. 2.9 million according to census 1st June 1956
6. John Wilson
7. Esther Vanhomrigh, of Celbridge, Kildare
8. He commanded England's anti-aircraft defences
9. Painting
10. O'Sullivan Mór
11. 'Lamh foistenach abu'
12. The gentle hand to victory
13. O'Sullivan Beare
14. The first Victoria Cross of the war awarded to an Irish navy man
15. Charlesfort, Kells, Co. Meath

Specials   (page 72)

1. August
2. The Claddagh Ring
3. The sale of the children of the poor as meat
4. River Arrow
5. The Farmers' Party, which ceased in 1960s
6. A collection of poems ('lays') by Sir William Ferguson
7. A 1920s rugby player
8. Ireland's caves and underground caverns
9. Winston Churchill
10. A village in Kilkenny
11. Cowhide, leather
12. Marty Morrissey, commentator, on Kilkenny's defeat of Wexford in Croke Park
13. National Park
14. 'To Whom It Concerns'
15. Dave Perry, originally from Northern Ireland

Sport   (page 73)

1. Once
2. Garryowen
3. 'Mighty Mouse'
4. 1980
5. Flyweight
6. Bantamweight
7. 1992
8. Welterweight
9. 1992
10. Hammer throw
11. Peter McParland
12. Jack Charlton
13. Stephen McPhail
14. Hurling
15. 1992

Natural History   *(page 74)*

1. Butterflies from all over the world
2. 4004 BC
3. He introduced the concept of 'critical temperatures'
4. William Parsons
5. 'Large stone' - describing the construction of the monuments
6. Peter Woulfe (Prokofiev wrote the music for Peter and the Wolf)
7. The Woulfe Bottle, a 2-necked glass container for safe handling of chemicals
8. 1727 in Dublin. He died in 1803
9. Sir Joseph Larmor
10. Lucasian Professor of Mathematics, Cambridge
11. Co. Wexford - two towns separated by one letter and several miles
12. The age of the Earth
13. Anemometer (windspeed gauge)
14. Trinity College, Dublin
15. In his father's Church of Ireland rectory, Navan, in 1774

Geography   *(page 75)*

1. 13.5 miles
2. Emain, 'the Navan', close to Armagh city
3. Myrtle Grove, Youghal
4. Portlaoise
5. Ballymena
6. Co. Kerry
7. In Sligo County Museum
8. Near Duncannon in Co. Wexford - in the 18th century, it was home to European gold- and silversmiths
9. Brandon Mountain
10. 300 metres
11. Dublin's oldest cemetery
12. Kilkenny
13. Strang fjord, or 'strong ford' - as described by the Vikings
14. Carlow
15. Kilkenny

History   *(page 76)*

1. Executed by firing squad May 12th 1916
2. 1st January 1801, under the Act of Union
3. Asgard
4. For their habit of scraping a steel tooth comb across a person's flesh as punishment
5. The first pleasure boat race in Ireland under rules
6. Transportation of Irish prisoners to Australia
7. Bowling Alley, Westminster
8. Ruari O'Connor
9. Norman-settled land, and 'wild Irish' land
10. Buildings in Georgian Dublin, as architects
11. 1937
12. Sir Roger Casement
13. Harland & Wolff
14. Girona
15. 'Germany calling, Germany calling...'

People   *(page 77)*

1. Gracie Fields, famous English actress and singer
2. Gore-Booth
3. General Sir Frederick 'Tim' Pile
4. Lady Jane Francesca Wilde
5. Oscar Wilde
6. Karl Marx ('drink is the curse of the working classes')

7. Adams
8. Professor of Natural Philosophy
9. 1747, died 1812
10. Protestant
11. 4.39 million according to census 2nd April 1911
12. Iseult (Tristram and Isolde)
13. 'Young' or Junior, as in Séan Óg
14. Richard Martin
15. Healer 'iceadh' in Irish

Specials   *(page 78)*

1. 18th century secret societies
2. A system of security for tenants, fair rent and tenure of land
3. A poisonous plant
4. A 'bobby' was a term for 19th century English police, a 'peeler' was its Irish counterpart
5. Sir Robert Peel
6. Sailing ships built by Harland & Wolff for a Mr Corry
7. The world's first 'Industrial Fishing School'
8. Jonah Barrington
9. A play written by Charles Macklin
10. Eamon de Valera
11. Master McGrath
12. He won 3 Waterloo Cups, and was a greyhound
13. William Joyce (Lord Haw-Haw), James Joyce
14. A cromlech on Luganquilla
15. A sports newspaper

Sport   *(page 79)*

1. 1 Bronze
2. John Caldwell
3. René Libeer of France
4. The first modern Olympics in 1896
5. New York competed for the first time
6. Richard Dunne
7. Steve Finnan
8. Lee Valley
9. 18th November, 1880
10. Queen's Hotel, Belfast
11. Cliftonville
12. 1890
13. Soccer
14. Rugby
15. A monocle

Television   *(page 80)*

1. *This Is Your Life*
2. TnaG
3. *Tolka Row*
4. *Glenroe*
5. 21st July 1955
6. Mary McAleese
7. RTÉ
8. The Angelus bells ring
9. *Z-cars*
10. Miles O'Brien
11. Pauline McLynn
12. Tony Doyle (Mr Fitzgerald) is the father of Susannah Doyle (Joy) in *Drop the Dead Donkey*
13. Stephen Thompkinson, as Damien and Father Peter Clifford
14. *Remington Steele*
15. Dublin city

Industry *(page 81)*

1. They produced bicycles and Dunlop's new tyres for Dunlop himself
2. Arthur Guinness
3. 1966
4. It rammed and sank and German U-boat in the First World War
5. Ulster, Munster, Leinster, Connaught
6. Ireland
7. Cultivation of oysters
8. Ebenezer Pike
9. Fertilizer
10. U-103
11. 1958
12. They were both occupied during the Easter Rising
13. Yahoo, from *Gulliver's Travels*
14. Donegal Tweed
15. Henry McIlhenny

Geography *(page 82)*

1. Tunbridge Wells, England, 1886
2. Kilkenny
3. From 'bretesche', Anglo-Norman wooden towers erected after 1170 Norman invasion
4. Slieve Donard
5. nr. Temple Douglas, Co. Donegal
6. Limerick
7. Ennis
8. Sligo
9. Roscommon, Ireland on May 17, 1911
10. Carlow
11. London, 11th December 1905
12. After 13th century Welsh settlers, of the family Joyce
13. Co. Waterford
14. New York
15. Co. Offaly

History *(page 83)*

1. Dublin Castle, as part of a small 'rebellion'
2. 6
3. Charles Stewart Parnell
4. Lunatic asylum
5. Dal Riada
6. 1592
7. To mark the visit of King George VI and his Queen
8. 43
9. None
10. Norway
11. The mixing of English colonists and Irish people, their language and law
12. Richard Jones
13. 1922
14. First World War
15. Fionn uisg - 'clear stream'

Music *(page 84)*

1. Moloko
2. 1996
3. *Robin of Sherwood, Harry's Game*
4. Philomena Begley
5. Ronan Keating
6. 1970

7. 7 times (to 2001)
8. Paul Harrington and Charlie McGettigan
9. 1907
10. *Finnegans Wake*
11. *A Clockwork Orange*
12. The Wolfe Tones
13. The harp
14. Carrick-on-Suir, Co. Tipperary
15. 'Athenry'

People (page 85)

1. John Millington
2. Barry Fitzgerald
3. Mairead Corrigan and Betty Williams
4. 1977 Nobel Prize for Peace
5. Padraig Pearse
6. A humourist/cartoonist
7. According to the Four Masters, 'he saw, he thought, St. Brigid in the act of killing him'
8. Irish
9. Earl of Erne
10. Edward Fitzgibbon of Limerick, born 1803
11. Catholic students
12. Temperance campaigner
13. Total abstinence societies
14. Joe Sheridan, in 1943
15. Galway Royal Mail line

Specials (page 86)

1. Someone imitating the short hairstyle and manners of a French Republican
2. Following the visit of King George VI
3. Limerick lace
4. 'More Irish than the Irish'
5. Brogue
6. Trinity College, Cambridge
7. A Canadian Pacific liner, it sank after a collision in the St. Lawrence seaway with the deaths of over 1000 people
8. The first commercial salmon fishery
9. In the manufacture of soap and glass
10. It was a good source of carbonate of soda
11. An Irish fascist organisation
12. A law stating that English parliament could pass laws which were binding in Ireland
13. A political movement
14. The ancient Great Road, linking Dublin with the west coast
15. A climbing route on Luggala, Co. Wicklow

Sport (page 87)

1. 21 a side
2. One, but that was a Gold
3. 5, one gold, one silver, three bronze
4. 2, one silver, one bronze
5. 1984
6. 2 hours, 9 minutes, 56 seconds
7. Patrick O'Callaghan, 1928-32
8. Hugh Russell
9. Hungary's Janos Varadi
10. Silver
11. Jose Casamayor of Cuba
12. Bantamweight
13. If a player's grandparents were Irish, that player is eligible to play for Ireland
14. Manchester United
15. The All Blacks

Theatre   (page 88)

1. Brian Friel
2. JM Synge
3. Ballymena, County Antrim
4. Joxer Daley in *Juno and the Paycock*
5. *The Plough and the Stars* (The Starry Plough)
6. Juno Boyle
7. George Bernard Shaw
8. Irish National Theatre
9. An Irish pronunciation of the word 'peacock'
10. Paris, France
11. Durban, South Africa, Nov. 26, 1910
12. Lady Gregory, Edward Martyn, George Moore
13. *Happy Days*
14. Samuel Beckett
15. John B. Keane

Geography   (page 89)

1. Marble Arch Caves
2. Larne, Co. Antrim
3. Tralee
4. Kilkenny
5. Dublin
6. Ballytore Co. Kildare in 1874
7. South Georgia, an island in the South Atlantic
8. Kilkenny
9. Drumcliffe churchyard, Co. Sligo
10. Cork
11. Lough Neagh
12. Cloughjordan, Tipperary
13. Donegal
14. Ulster
15. Lurgan, Co. Armagh, 25th December 1881

History   (page 90)

1. Irish Republican Brotherhood
2. Irish Republican Army
3. Irish Citizen Army
4. 17th March 1858
5. Canada, occupying parts of the town of Port Erie
6. Royal Irish Constabulary
7. Royal Ulster Constabulary
8. Garda Siochana
9. Belfast City Hall
10. Great Northern Railway
11. 1591
12. 1908
13. Sitric, Norse King of Dublin
14. 1920
15. The *Edward*

People   (page 91)

1. Martin Cahill
2. An area in Belfast made up of Jerusalem Street, Palestine Street and Damascus Street
3. Samuel Beckett
4. 15th January 1986
5. December 1998
6. Irish railways

7. Lord Wavertree
8. Michael O'Clery, Farfasa O'Mulchrony, Peregrine O'Clery and Peregrine O'Dingenan
9. Harry Ferguson
10. Father John Murphy
11. Godard van Reede, born 1644
12. George Berkeley
13. John Dawson
14. Sir Edward Lutyens
15. Gertrude Jekyll

Religion (page 92)

1. Bishop Michael Cox
2. Gold
3. His head
4. In a shrine at St. Peter's Church, Drogheda, Co. Louth
5. Cardinal Paparo, 1150
6. Henry II, by a proclamation 'Laudabiliter'
7. He was a Presbyterian
8. Tassach, a disciple who founded a church in Raholp, Co. Down
9. 1st February
10. The Vikings - 'From the fury of the Norsemen Lord deliver us'
11. An airport
12. The Irish Brigade of the British Army
13. 1142
14. Cistercians
15. 1829

Specials (page 93)

1. Sale and importation of contraceptives
2. 23rd August 1916, with the introduction of Greenwich Mean Time (GMT)
3. A lifeboat station
4. Irish Bicycle Polo Association
5. Ireland (map co-ordinates)
6. *c.* 250ft basalt cliffs near Islandmagee, Co. Antrim
7. Fastnet Yacht Race
8. Reclaimed alluvial land
9. *Frankenstein*, by Mary Shelley
10. A limestone lake, which dries in summer, to appear again after heavy rainfall
11. Shannon Airport
12. An ancient hide covered, cylindrical boat
13. A workers'movement in 19th-century Pennsylvania
14. Royal Dublin Society
15. An Irish potato recipe

Sport (page 94)

1. 1894
2. The London-Sydney marathon
3. Northern Football Union
4. February 1879
5. 'Quiz' is another, obsolete name for a monocle
6. Cricket
7. The West Indies
8. Sion Mills, Co. Derry
9. Women's cricket
10. 1936
11. Rock climbing
12. Wales and Ireland
13. Ireland, by 3-0
14. Rhyl in Wales
15. Handball

Theatre _ (page 95)

1. Pegeen Mike
2. 'Captain' Jack Boyle
3. Douglas Hyde (Casadh an tSúgain) 1901
4. Jean Butler
5. *Playboy of the Western World*
6. Dion Boucicault, *The Colleen Bawn*
7. Lennox Robinson
8. Sean O'Casey
9. *Playboy of the Western World*
10. Killyclogher, Co. Tyrone
11. Sean O'Casey
12. Philadelphia, *Philadelphia Here I Come*
13. Brendan Behan
14. 39
15. Liam O'Flaherty

Politics (page 96)

1. 30th June 1981
2. 2
3. Martin McGuinness
4. 17
5. 1931
6. Eamon de Valera
7. 1905
8. 1923
9. 1933. It changed its name
10. He was Taoiseach
11. Rev. Ian Paisley
12. 'Ourselves Alone'
13. Democratic Unionist Party
14. Fine Gael
15. Colonel John O'Mahony (1815-77)

Arts (page 97)

1. *The Nation*, in October 1842
2. John Mitchel
3. John Hewitt
4. Evie Hone
5. In *The Nation* newspaper
6. Dame Ninette De Valois
7. A system of colour photography
8. Baltiboys, Ireland, 1898
9. Edris Stannus
10. *Pennsylvania Packet*
11. He was an Irish artist
12. *An emigrant ship, Dublin bay, sunset*
13. Phoebe Anna Traquair
14. As a sculptor (1760-1822)
15. As a portrait painter (1756-1822)

Films (page 98)

1. *Schindler's List*, based on *Schindler's Ark*, by Thomas Kinealy
2. *Angela's Ashes*
3. *A Life Less Ordinary*
4. *The Snapper*
5. *Into the West*
6. Pink Floyd's *The Wall*

7. Stephen Rea
8. Will Danaher ('Red' Will)
9. Mary Kate Danaher
10. A boxer
11. *This Sporting Life*
12. *My Left Foot*
13. Scottish
14. Helen Mirren
15. Michael Collins

Geography

(page 99)

1. Maghera, 1729
2. Cork
3. Mullingar
4. Donegal
5. Lough Foyle
6. Iniskeen, Co. Monaghan
7. Cahir and Clonmel
8. At the tip of Toormore Bay, Co. Cork
9. Athy
10. The Tolka
11. Meath
12. Clare
13. Wicklow
14. St George's Channel, stretch of water
15. Longford

History

(page 100)

1. Monster meetings
2. Fighting in battle
3. A 'sham fight' commemorating the Battle of the Boyne 1690
4. Valentia Island
5. To enable communication between Europe and America
6. Youghal
7. 1846
8. 1908
9. Edward Carson
10. John A. Costello, 14th November 1948
11. The Dublin Lockout of August 1913
12. The city's Jewish community
13. Upper Sackville Street
14. Horatio Nelson
15. 1940

People

(page 101)

1. Natasha Richardson
2. Sir Robert John Le Mesurier McClure
3. Daniel O'Connell
4. Michael O'Donovan
5. King Haakon IV
6. Miss Linch, as stewardess on board the Sirius, April 1838
7. WB Yeats
8. Éamon de Valera
9. James Connolly, 7th July 1900
10. John Morley, Liberal MP, 12th May 1902
11. An Irish widow involved in protests against landlords in the 1840s
12. 'Dove of the Church'
13. Richard Fitzralph, Archbishop of Armagh
14. 'Lord of the horses'
15. Herons

ANSWERS

Specials (page 102)

1. 15
2. Irish soldiers serving in the Irish Brigade of the French army in the 1690s
3. A walking stick, or sometimes a 'cudgel', made from blackthorn wood
4. The woods around Shillelagh in Co. Wicklow was a great source of such wood
5. The County Down and Ward Union packs
6. Equal 44th in Olympic medal ranking
7. A marriage which held together for "only a year and a day"
8. Half of the world's population of Greenland white-fronted geese (6,000)
9. 1959
10. Cats so fierce that, when they fought, there was nothing left of them but tails - hence 'they fought like Kilkenny cats'.
11. They are Irish dances
12. The labourers who dug 'navigation channels' on Englsih canals in 18th century
13. James Bond
14. A large concert venue in Dublin
15. Another name for Irish potato bread

Sport (page 103)

1. GAA teams visited America en masse
2. 328 miles
3. 1903
4. A yacht race off Kingstown in 1898
5. 15th February 1875
6. Kennington Oval, London
7. 1894
8. Two of the players went on to win the Victoria Cross during the Boer War
9. Willie Anderson
10. Triple Crown
11. Joe Comiskey, who was doctor to the Irish Olympic squad
12. Willie John McBride
13. In his final home international
14. 1921
15. Liam McCarthy

Natural History (page 104)

1. The badger
2. The Burren Orchid
3. Irish Water Spaniel
4. Deerhound
5. Irish Wolfhound
6. Kerry Blue
7. *Skibberreen Eagle*
8. Robert Boyle, 1627-91
9. 'the volume of a fixed quantity of a gas at a constant temperature is inversely proportional to its pressure'
10. 'Leviathan'
11. University of Ulster, Coleraine
12. Lucasian Professor of Mathematics, Cambridge
13. Francis Beaufort, who recommended that Charles Darwin be part of the *Beagle*'s voyage in the 1830s
14. The Beaufort Scale
15. The lark - Mullary Cross' Irish name is Mullach Lámhraighe; Lavrock's Height (lavrock or laverock is the lark)

Literature (page 105)

1. Brooklyn, N.Y., on Aug. 19, 1930
2. Brian Moore
3. An honorary CBE (Commander, Order of the British Empire)
4. Landlords of Irish property who were not themselves resident in Ireland
5. *A Portrait of the Artist as a Young Man*
6. Gerald Griffin

7. James Plunkett
8. To let down his country
9. Derek Dougan
10. Walk through Ireland (*A Frenchman's walk through Ireland 1796-7*)
11. The apostrophe was removed
12. November 1713
13. *Tristram Shandy*
14. *Under the Eye of the Clock*
15. Tim

Films   (page 106)

1. George Best
2. *Out of Sight*
3. *Toy Story*
4. *The Long Kiss Goodnight*
5. 'Year'
6. 7
7. 0
8. *Miller's Crossing*
9. Richard Harris
10. Mary McGuckian
11. John Lynch
12. Michael Collins
13. Sam Neill, who starred in *Jurassic Park* and *Omen III - The Final Conflict*
14. Tara Fitzgerald
15. Between Victor McLaglen and John Wayne in *The Quiet Man*

Geography   (page 107)

1. Cruachain, Rathcrogan, Co. Roscommon
2. Wexford, Co. Wexford
3. Galway
4. Trim
5. Kilkenny
6. Sligo
7. Laois
8. An Mágh, the plan
9. Devil's Backbone
10. Slievenamon, Co. Tipperary
11. 375 sq km
12. Donegal
13. Co. Wexford
14. Tipperary
15. Edinburgh

History   (page 108)

1. Between 1794-98
2. Carlisle Bridge
3. In 1882
4. 1902
5. Within 97 miles
6. 1734
7. 'Bloody Sunday'
8. 1814
9. The abdication of King Edward VIII
10. Vladimir Illyich Lenin
11. April 24, 1906, New York, N.Y., U.S.
12. William Joyce
13. 'Lord Haw-Haw'
14. William Joyce was executed as a traitor although he was not British
15. St. Ruth and Ginkel

People

(page 109)

1. Colonel St. Leger, namesake of the famous classic horse race
2. Sir Robert Peel
3. 24th March 1909
4. Lord Palmerston, in 1842
5. C. Day Lewis
6. He won a seat in House of Commons, but did not take his seat (North Roscommon)
7. Zachary
8. Last Sunday in July
9. 'J'aime mon Dieu, mon Roi et mon patri'
10. I love my God, my King and my Country
11. Wolff
12. Edward Harland and Gustav Wolff
13. 1895
14 1913
15. The MacDermots

Specials

(page 110)

1. Douglas Hyde, noted Gaelic scholar
2. It was run by Tom Crean, Antarctic explorer
3. Trinity College, Dublin
4. Gannet, the seabird
5. An offshore island important for nesting seabirds
6. Theft and villainy - a 'tory' was a thief
7. A member of the British Conservative Party - a name adopted in the eighteenth century
8. A collection of Irish literature in the 17th century, such as The Annals
9. 00 353
10. A method of torture, involving burning molten tar
11. A French proclamation of 1798, issued after their landing in Mayo
12. After 1821
13. Liner *Titanic*
14. Its Bachelors' Festival
15. Ulster Society for the Prevention of Cruelty to Animals

Sport

(page 111)

1. Arsenal
2. Jimmy Dunne, 1930, 1971
3. Michelle Smith
4. An automobile race
5. 1943
6. 1960
7. Down
8. 9
9. Gaelic football and hurling
10. Galway and Derry, Kilkenny and Clare
11. Tim Long and Brendan Kean
12. Erin's Hope and Clan na Gael
13. Stephen Roche
14. Handball
15. Handball

Geography

(page 112)

1. As a reservoir, and source of water for Belfast
2. Naas
3. Lifford
4. Armagh
5. Spas or springs at Lisdoonvarna, Co. Clare
6. It once meant 'place of the thistles'

7. Connemara
8. It was established by the London Company of Drapers during the Ulster Plantation
9. Derry
10. Monaghan
11. Utrecht, Netherlands
12. 3
13. 1853
14. Grianán of Aileach
15. On the River Blackwater

History *(page 113)*

1. 26th February 1962
2. Aireacht
3. 29th December 1937
4. The League of Nations
5. 18th April 1949
6. 22nd June 1921
7. Adolf Hitler, April 1945
8. 16th November 1965
9. 26th June 1963
10. United Nations Security Council
11. 17th June 1959
12. 14th December 1955
13. 8th August 1923
14. 10th September 1923
15. 17th February 1922

People *(page 114)*

1. Archbishop Thomas Croke
2. George French, from Roscommon, in 1873
3. Oscar Wilde
4. 3.53 million according to census 21nd April 1991
5. Jack B. Yeats, who wrote poetry under this pseudonym
6. Edward De Valera
7. Goidelic
8. Aer Lingus
9. O'Brien, Earl of Thomond
10. 'Lamh laidir an nachtar' or 'Lamh Laidir an Uachtar'
11. The strong hand uppermost
12. 'Lamh dearg Eirin'
13. The Red Hand to Victory
14. He was an architect
15. George Bernard Shaw

Specials *(page 115)*

1. The Velvet Strand, Co. Dublin, by Mollison in a Puss Moth
2. Altamont
3. Camogie
4. The long-extinct Irish Elk
5. Glenariff
6. A Celtic mother goddess
7. Irish tenants refused to have anything to do with their English landlord, named Boycott.
8. An Irish potato dish
9. Jacob's biscuits
10. Antrim's county GAA sides
11. Down
12. 0-20
13. British retreat from Castlebar to Athlone
14. Some troops covered a distance of 63 miles over a 27 hour period, on foot
15. Ballymany Stud, Newbridge, Co. Kildare

Geography (page 116)

1. The lands were confiscated from nobles who left Ireland in the Flight of the Earls
2. Kilternan, Co. Dublin
3. Tullamore
4. Cork
5. Tipperary
6. 4 miles south-west of Cape Clear, Co. Cork
7. Ballycastle, Co. Antrim
8. Armagh
9. Galway
10. Offaly
11. Carlingford, Co. Louth, in 1825
12. 'Pro fide regia, et patria pugno'
13. College Hill, Armagh city
14. In the grounds of the former monastery of All Hallows
15. Bally Sampson, 1745

Sport (page 117)

1. 1924
2. The Curragh
3. He failed to gain any points
4. Handball
5. Victor Le Fanu, son of Sheridan
6. 5 years of age
7. The Derby
8. George Best
9. Patrick J. Ryan
10. Hammer-throw
11. International Rugby
12. Twenty-nine
13. Sixty-seven
14. 'Danno' O'Keeffe, Kerry goalkeeper
15. Rinty Monaghan

Geography (page 118)

1. John Dunlop, born in Strabane, Co. Down
2. Wicklow
3. Islandmagee, Co. Antrim
4. Tayto Castle
5. Fermanagh
6. Cavan
7. Waterford
8. Hollow place
9. An ancient stone cicle
10. Donegal
11. Kingstown and Holyhead in Wales
12. Wolfe Tone Street
13. Pierce's Table
14. 80 feet
15. Donegal

Specials (page 119)

1. The first steam ship to cross the Atlantic, 1838, from Passage West, Co. Cork
2. Dried seaweed
3. Salmon
4. An Irish ceílí dance
5. 83.09 miles per hour
6. Anonymous letters critical of England's treatment of Ireland

7. Jonathan Swift
8. A 'fictional author', created by author Patrick McCabe
9. The Wren Boys
10. They were ships involved in the French landings in 1798
11. Hint
12. Lattice-beam bridge
13. The vessel *Wild Duck* was renamed *Lexington*, captained by Barry
14. The Academy Award
15. A racecourse near Dublin

Sport (page 120)

1. 1992
2. Padraig Harrington
3. Kiawah Island, South Carolina, USA
4. Éamon de Valera
5. Pádraig MacNamee
6. The football burst
7. Cork and Kerry
8. No ball was available
9. Galway was unopposed in first, in second Galway was awarded the title
10. The 1993 Sam Maguire
11. Henry Downey
12. Norman Whiteside
13. Hurling
14. Kilkenny
15. Dave McAuley

Geography (page 121)

1. Aughrim, Avoca, Gold Mines
2. Armagh
3. Roscommon
4. West Virginia
5. Killarney
6. Ireland's main grey seal breeding ground
7. St Patrick's Church of Ireland
8. Sellafield
9. Sligo
10. Kerry
11. Wales
12. 125 feet
13. Knockmany Passage Grave
14. Co. Mayo
15. Poddle

Specials (page 122)

1. Cork
2. The collection of Sir Hans Sloane
3. A court case in 1617 decided that it must be Irish, for there were no snakes on the island
4. *Na Frasa,* the showers (possibly of blood)
5. An estuary area, important for wading birds and other wildfowl
6. Mountains in Co. Kerry
7. A type of shoe, once worn on the Aran Islands
8. Land speed record
9. Whiskey
10. £5,000,000
11. Romania (due to his charity work)
12. Traditional wailing as a sign of intense grief
13. Orange yeomen in 1798
14. Secretary of State for War and the Colonies in April 1834
15. A motor rally circuit

Sport   *(page 123)*

1. 26th July 1987
2. Soccer
3. Rugby - for exceptional contribution to Irish rugby
4. New Zealand's All Blacks
5. Ramelton, Co. Donegal
6. Camogie
7. She played in both finals on the same day in 1973
8. Kathleen Mills
9. Munster
10. Leinster
11. 18 years, 19 days
12. He was English
13. Danny Blanchflower
14. Dawson Stelfox
15. 1986

Geography   *(page 124)*

1. Devil's Bit Mountain, Co. Tipperary
2. Kildare
3. Co. Kilkenny
4. Co. Dublin
5. Laois
6. Belfast
7. Antrim in Ireland, Argyllshire in Scotland
8. Seven Sisters
9. Leighlinbridge, Carlow, 1820-93
10. Queenstown (Cobh)
11. London, March 1918
12. Stafford Street, no.44
13. Donegal
14. Large's Landing Place
15. Inishmore island, 1896

Specials   *(page 125)*

1. Giant's Causeway
2. Yellow man
3. German Protestant settlers, in 1709
4. 140 feet
5. Sir John McNeill
6. Queenstown - the emigration which took place from this port
7. January 9th and January 10th, 1928
8. Two birth certificates were issued
9. Irish sea voyages (it was a paddle steamer)
10. Irish Loyal and Patriotic Union, founded in 1885
11. Willis O'Brien, animator of 'King Kong'
12. Sex
13. Crean and Harvey
14. A term of abuse for rugby officials
15. Garryowen

Specials   *(page 126)*

1. Co. Armagh, 1795
2. 17th March 1762
3. 17th March 461
4. They had completed the first transatlantic powered flight
5. Lotto
6. In the Vatican

7. The creation of a new, meaningless word, and encourage its common use in 24 hours (apocryphal story)
8. Quiz
9. Theatre manager
10. St Brendan is supposed to have discovered America in the 6th century, 900 years before Columbus
11. Christian Brothers
12. Ascents in the Twelve Bens
13. A handball court
14. As a singer
15. Zog

Sport   (page 127)

1. 10 years
2. 5
3. 9
4. None
5. Rugby
6. England
7. Formula One motor racing
8. Belfast
9. 4th May 1946
10. Joint runner-up in the 1982 World Drivers Championship
11. Ballymoney, Co. Antrim
12. 25th February 1952
13. Association (football - soccer)
14. 13-0 in favour of the opposition
15. Gaelic

Geography   (page 128)

1. Carlow
2. 197 metres
3. Westmeath
4. Dublin
5. Rutland Island
6. A holy well
7. Bruff, Limerick
8. Liscannor, Co. Clare
9. Galway - St.John's, Newfoundland
10. Ireland's Eye - it is a sea cliff
11. In the books of Patrick McCabe
12. Slane Castle
13. Waterville Promontory
14. Bruree, Co. Limerick
15. 'Island of holly'

Sport   (page 129)

1. 1929
2. 3rd July 2000
3. Celtic (Glasgow Celtic)
4. Hockey
5. 103
6. Hockey
7. Stephen Martin
8. A modern form of the ancient competitions held between tribes - the 'Irish Olympics'
9. 1924
10. 4 years
11. Leopardstown
12. Generous
13. Sammy McIlroy
14. Lawrie McMenemy
15. Mick McCarthy

Geography (page 130)

1. Wicklow, near Avoca
2. Clonmel
3. The sand on its shore is made up of fragments of coralline algae, forming 'coral' beaches
4. Tyrone
5. Longford
6. Shannon
7. Limerick
8. Lough Leane
9. Lismore Castle, Waterford, 1662
10. Belfast, in 1905
11. Moville, Co. Derry
12. Isle of Man, from Manannan
13. Dunganstown, Co. Wexford
14. Donegal
15. Baldonnel aerodrome, Co. Dublin

Sport (page 131)

1. Norway
2. Formula One motor-racing
3. Manchester United and Republic of Ireland
4. Horse-racing
5. Leicester City
6. Kevin Heffernan
7. London
8. 1923 in Dublin
9. Commissioner Eoin O'Duffy
10. It was considered unfair competition (members were then transferred throughout the country)
11. 1947
12. Larry Kiely of Tipperary
13. Dr Edwin Fitzgibbon, priest, Philosophy Professor, University College, Cork 1911-36
14. Ladies Gaelic Football Association
15. 1974, Hayes Hotel, Thurles, Tipperary

Geography (page 132)

1. Cap Martin on the French Riviera
2. Rockall, an outcrop in the Atlantic Ocean
3. Arlington National Cemetery, Virginia
4. Cork
5. Leitrim
6. Wexford
7. 240 miles (390km)
8. Inishmore, Inishmaan, Inisheer
9. Lionsden
10. Lower Lough Erne in Fermanagh
11. Ballynahowe, Co. Galway
12. Galway - it's in Connemara
13. Wicklow
14. Armagh, Co. Armagh
15. Belfast

Geography (page 133)

1. Lough Lean
2. Down
3. Kildare
4. Paris, France
5. Swanlinbar
6. Co. Kerry

7. Baillieborough, Co. Meath
8. A windmill, bulilt in 1846
9. Camus
10. An 18th century canal linking Belfast with Lough Neagh
11. In the Mourne Mountains - it is a climb
12. Rope bridge
13. Dublin
14. Ballymena, Co. Antrim
15. Kerry

Specials   (page 134)

1. Jupiter (although the Captain is not comparable)
2. Finn MacCool scooped up earth, throwing it into the Irish Sea, creating the Isle of Man
3. Drowned the last of Ireland's snakes
4. 900 years
5. Aodh, Fionnuala, Conn and Fiachra
6. 26
7. Distribution of clan land for a fixed number of years
8. It is a form taken by a departing soul
9. A magical spear
10. Grey of Macha, Black of Saingield
11. Forgall the Wily, a druid
12. Uath, the Stranger
13. That Cuchlainn could behead him only if Uath was allowed to do the same
14. A hill in the Glens of Antrim
15. Joxer Daly, from Juno and the Paycock

Geography   (page 135)

1. The Burren
2. Annalong, Co. Down
3. Antrim
4. Limerick
5. Mayo
6. St Mogue
7. Big island, middle island, east island
8. Dublin
9. Lough Gur
10. Two barrow-graves
11. A dolmen
12. Lurgan, Co. Armagh, in 1654
13. Dublin's fair city
14. Lee
15. Garinish

Specials   (page 136)

1. Jordan - Eddie Jordan
2. Her cloak
3. It once covered about 12 acres
4. Tyrone
5. 5th Marquis of Lansdowne
6. 'St Patrick's Purgatory'
7. 3,000
8. Bishop of Armagh - real name Terence Donnelly, he ministered in secret during the time of the Penal Laws.
9. His footprints (carved into the rock where he stood)
10. Strule
11. Pirates from Algiers, led by a man from Dungarvan
12. John Alcock and Arthur Brown
13. Parick Pearse
14. Seamus Heaney
15. French

Geography (page 137)

1. Newtownbarry
2. Louth
3. Dunsink Observatory
4. Dungarvan, Waterford, 1903
5. Salzburg, Austria
6. Dun Laoghaire
7. *The World*
8. USPCA Centre
9. Cork
10. Richard Alfred Milliken, The Groves of Blarney
11. Belturbet, Co. Cavan
12. Kilkeel and Hilltown, Co Down
13. Charles Stewart Parnell
14. Transatlantic wireless telegrams
15. The Planetarium

INVISIBLE HEROES

SURVIVORS OF TRAUMA
AND HOW THEY HEAL

Belleruth Naparstek

Foreword by Robert C. Scaer, M.D.

BANTAM BOOKS

INVISIBLE HEROES
A Bantam Book

PUBLISHING HISTORY
Bantam hardcover edition published September 2004
Bantam trade paperback edition / January 2006

Published by
Bantam Dell
A Division of Random House, Inc.
New York, New York

Book design by Glen Edelstein

Library of Congress Catalog Card Number: 2004046171

Bantam Books and the rooster colophon
are registered trademarks of Random House, Inc.

ISBN-13: 978-0-553-38374-4
ISBN-10: 0-553-38374-4

Printed in the United States of America
Published simultaneously in Canada

www.bantamdell.com

BVG 10 9 8 7 6 5 4